"Filled with sensible advice, *Teaching Your Children Good Manners* gives frazzled parents the practical tools they need to teach their kids—whatever their ages—to treat others with respect, kindness, and consideration. And really, what's more important than that?"

Armin Brott

Author of *The Expectant Father: Facts, Tips, and Advice for Dads-to-Be* and *A Dad's Guide to the Toddler Years.*

"Wow! *Teaching Your Children Good Manners* is the best survival book for parents I have read. Everyone talks about social skills, finally a creative, practical, fun, developmentally appropriate book focuses on teaching skills every child needs. *Teaching Your Children Good Manners* is a must read for parents of children of all ages. Follow these suggestions and your friends will be amazed at your children's maturity. And, you will be amazed at how their new skills help them succeed."

Dr. Ken West

Author of *The Shelbys Need Help! A Choose-Your-Own Solution and Adventure Book*

TEACHING YOUR CHILDREN GOOD MANNERS

a *Go Parents!* guide™

Nomad Press
A division of Nomad Communications
10 9 8 7 6 5 4 3 2 1
Copyright © 2001 Nomad Communications

ISBN 0-9659258-1-1
Library of Congress Cataloging-in-Publication data available.

Questions regarding the ordering of this book should be addressed to
The Independent Publishers Group
814 N. Franklin St.
Chicago IL 60610

Cover artwork and interior illustrations by Charles Woglom, Big Hed Designs
Design by David Morin
Edited by Susan Kahan

Nomad Press, PO Box 875, Norwich, VT 05055

To Josh, who appreciates good manners.

—LB

Acknowledgements

This book is the work of many people, all of whom showed incredible patience (and beautiful manners) throughout the long process of research, writing, and production. I want to thank Rachel Benoit, Leslie Connolly, Leslie Johnston, and Kristen Wilson, who provided information, advice, and personal anecdotes that are the foundation for much of the book. Many thanks to Charlie Woglom at Big Hed Designs for his great illustrations. Thanks also to everyone at Nomad Press for their help, hard work, and enduring good humor, especially Alex Kahan for his ideas, Susan Hale for her expertise at editing, and David Morin for his terrific book design. Finally, thanks to Richard, Sasha, Noah, and Simon, the inspiration for writing a book about manners in the first place. Please chew with your mouths closed.

—LB

I would like to thank my parents, Tom and Martha, for their support, understanding, and humor. My accomplishments are a reflection of your love and parenting skills. I would also like to acknowledge Staci "Mae" and Jeff, two extraordinary people who I am fortunate to have in my life. Thanks for being there. Finally, it is with appreciation that I acknowledge Lauri Berkenkamp for her hard work and dedication. Her belief in the subject made this book possible.

—SA

Table of Contents

This was *not* part of the job description.

You were thrilled at the prospect of a lovely family dinner out at a restaurant with your perfect, adorable children. Less than an hour later your table looks like a battlefield—and your side lost. Your three-year old suddenly decides she's finished with dinner, gets down, and walks away to investigate other tables. Her six-year-old brother is using his utensils as weapons to fight an invisible foe, with all the loud sound effects you'd expect from a battle on the Dark Planet. Meanwhile, your thirteen-year old is sulking in a corner because you had the nerve to ask him to sit up straight. Everyone in the restaurant must be watching you, thinking you're a terrible parent who hasn't bothered to teach a thing about good manners. You vow never to go out to dinner again.

Sound familiar? Don't worry—help is at hand. **Teaching Your Children Good Manners** is a book designed to help you teach your children the basics of good manners in a straightforward, common-sense way through concrete ideas, and fun games and activities. All the advice and information in each chapter is geared toward age-appropriate levels, because you certainly can't expect the same manners from a three-year old as you can from a thirteen-year old, regardless of how similarly they may behave at times.

Why Teach Good Manners?

Let's face it, good manners are important—they demonstrate respect for others. Manners are simply unwritten rules of conduct that make the world a more pleasant place. Eating a meal with someone who chews loudly with his mouth open is disgusting. Sitting through a flight to Chicago with an eight-year old kicking the back of your seat the entire way is misery. We all want to live in a society where people are polite and respectful of others. We all want our children to make a good impression, whether it's over the phone or in an introduction. Think about this: teaching your children proper table manners now could pay off during that crucial job interview twenty years from now, which just happens to conclude with lunch. Good manners are good for your kids, and might even give them an advantage in life.

Good manners demonstrate respect for others, and make the world a more pleasant place.

How to Use This Book

This book should be used as a guide; the etiquette suggestions discussed here are those that are considered polite in the United States, although most are universal. It acknowledges that while raising kids is, indeed, serious business, it's also exasperating, fun, and often very funny—all at the same time. The advice and ideas for teaching kids the basics of proper social etiquette are offered from the viewpoint that kids are occasionally going to burp really loudly at the table, completely melt down at just the wrong moment, and often won't behave like any of those kids on TV sitcoms—unless you count *"The Simpsons."*

Teaching Your Children Good Manners is organized so that you can either read it straight through, or pick and choose the sections most useful to you at a given time. Each chapter tackles a different social circumstance and provides a brief outline of the appropriate manners for that situation. You'll find valuable advice on how to teach these manners to children of different ages, with age-appropriate games, activities, and ideas designed to reinforce the manners discussed. ***Questions & Answers*** that look at common situations and offer practical solutions are followed by a ***What to Expect*** section broken down by age.

Worried that your children will eat like cavemen forever? Read ***Chapter One: Don't Talk with Your Mouth Full*** for some advice and helpful hints about using utensils, appropriate dinner table conversation, and other manners at the table. ***Chapter Two: What Did You Just Say?*** offers some advice and ideas about appropriate language use, no matter how awkward the situation. If you're wondering how to introduce your children to the mysterious creatures known as grownups, read ***Chapter Three: I'd Like You to Meet . . .*** to learn how to help your kids meet and greet adults—and children.

Chapter Four: Hello, Who's This? focuses on phone manners, from taking and leaving messages to learning to answer the phone politely, while ***Chapter Five: It's My Party*** provides help with invitations, party manners, and writing the dreaded-but-necessary thank you note. Thinking of taking a trip with your children? Or simply going to the food store?

Turn to **Chapter Six: Quit Kicking My Seat** to brush up on manners in public places and while traveling. **Chapter Seven: We Rule! You Drool! Go Team!** tackles the timely issue of manners on the sports field.

At the end of every chapter you'll find guidelines broken down by age group for what to expect from your child in terms of the topic discussed in that chapter. Please note that these guidelines are based on very general developmental milestones and your child might be much more or less developmentally advanced, and therefore capable of more or less than the guidelines suggest.

Golden Rules for Teaching Manners

Whether you're the parent of a toddler and you want to get a head start on your child's social development, or have teenagers and want to reinforce the social skills you know they are capable of demonstrating, teaching your children good manners takes a lot of hard work and persistence. Keep in mind the following golden rules:

1. Model good behavior: You are your children's most important role model, and your actions will speak far louder than your words. So if you talk with your mouth full, or interrupt other people, your kids will too. Use this opportunity to pay attention to your own manners.

2. Plan for success: A little advance planning goes a long way toward helping your kids use good manners in social situations. You'll find lots of ideas throughout the book that will help you create opportunities for your children to learn and use good manners successfully.

3. Have high expectations but set realistic goals: Don't forget that kids can focus on only one or two new ideas at a time. When you are teaching or reinforcing manners in a particular setting, such as the dinner table or when answering the phone, focus on only one or two specific skills at a time. Once your kids have mastered those, move on to others. Build on the good things you have already taught them and progress from there.

4. Be patient: Good manners are just good habits that are learned and practiced over time. Your kids aren't going to learn them all at once, and they won't remember them all the time. But with encouragement and positive reinforcement, and lots of practice, your kids' good manners will eventually become automatic.

5. Have a sense of humor: Accidents will happen, food will be spilled, and social gaffes will be committed. Guaranteed. Keep smiling—remember that honing social skills takes a long time, and slip ups are inevitable. The embarrassing moments now will make funny stories in the future.

You are your kids' personal manners coach in the game of life—use **Teaching Your Children Good Manners** *as your playbook.*

Using the ideas in this book, you can set high standards for your kids and achieve results by offering them positive support and lots of encouragement, and by making it fun to learn good manners. Consider yourself their personal manners coach in the game of life, and use *Teaching Your Children Good Manners: a Go Parents! guide*™ as your playbook.

Your Approach to Teaching

Teaching your kids good manners is a long process, so you might as well get used to the idea that you'll be saying "Please use your fork" or "What's the magic word?" for many years to come. But remember that the way you approach teaching your children manners is almost as important as what you teach them.

Generally, taking a positive approach to teaching good manners will go a lot further than a daily harangue, and the more you model the kind of behavior you want your children to learn, the more likely they are to learn it.

Studies have shown that parents who set clear rules and high standards for their children, but are also flexible, explain why they made those rules, and emphasize rewards over punishment, will have the most success.

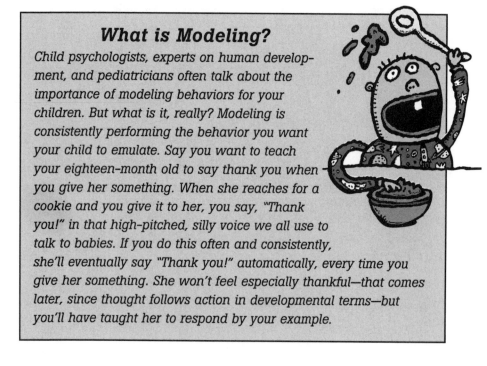

What is Modeling?

Child psychologists, experts on human development, and pediatricians often talk about the importance of modeling behaviors for your children. But what is it, really? Modeling is consistently performing the behavior you want your child to emulate. Say you want to teach your eighteen-month old to say thank you when you give her something. When she reaches for a cookie and you give it to her, you say, "Thank you!" in that high-pitched, silly voice we all use to talk to babies. If you do this often and consistently, she'll eventually say "Thank you!" automatically, every time you give her something. She won't feel especially thankful—that comes later, since thought follows action in developmental terms—but you'll have taught her to respond by your example.

DON'T TALK WITH YOUR MOUTH FULL:
manners at the TABLE

Every now and then you'll have a meal where everything goes right: your children are polite to you and each other, they sit in their seats, nothing gets spilled (or thrown), everyone likes what is being served, and you all actually converse with each other. It's like being on an episode of "The Waltons," and it's wonderful. This is the kind of meal you want to have every day, and this chapter will help you get there—one step at a time. It covers how to teach your kids the basics of good table manners, including setting the table and trying new foods. With practice and a lot of good humor, you and your family will have many more meals where you wish the cameras were rolling—or your own mother was there to notice what a good job you're doing.

The Basics

There's something about being part of a process that makes you care more about the end result. It's the same with kids and table manners. The more you can include your kids in the process of providing the meal—from choosing what to serve to making sure the table looks good—the more likely they'll want every aspect of it, including the way they behave at the table, to be just right. Encourage and allow your kids to get involved in the process of creating the meal, rather than simply showing up, and they'll be more likely to care about the end result.

Basic table manners covered in this chapter:

✳ Setting the table and helping clean up

✳ Sitting at the table and knowing when to start eating

✳ Reaching vs. passing

✳ Using utensils

✳ Talking at the table

✳ Being excused

How You Can Plan for Success

• *Warn your children that you'll be calling them for dinner (or to come help), well before you expect them. A 30-minute warning and then a 5-minute warning can prepare them for the transition from play or homework, giving them time to finish what they are doing.*

• *Involve your kids in meal planning and preparations.*

• *Prompt the behavior you expect clearly, but positively.*

• *Pick your battles—choose one or two skills to focus on at a time: you don't want dinner to be nag, nag, nag.*

• *Be patient! Using good table manners is really hard. Cheer the successes.*

Mission Possible

Older children can rotate their kitchen chores, so that one child sets the entire table one night (or for a week) and another clears. You may find that setting up a written schedule works best; it may help avoid the "it's your turn, no it's not" syndrome. Make sure the kids have input when setting up the schedule—they'll feel better about being roped into service when they have a say.

Getting Ready

Children from the age of four should be able to wash their hands by themselves before a meal. Teach your youngest children to wash their hands with soap. It is the single most important health practice your kids can learn—you've seen where those hands have been, and it's not likely anyone will want to share whatever they've been touching.

Remind your children that outdoor clothing is worn outdoors; they should remove their coats, hats and other gear—including video games, walkman, and baseball gloves—before coming to the table to eat. A good, easy-to-remember rule for kids of any age is "Come to the table with empty hands."

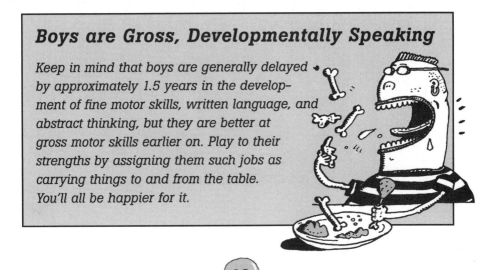

Boys are Gross, Developmentally Speaking

Keep in mind that boys are generally delayed by approximately 1.5 years in the development of fine motor skills, written language, and abstract thinking, but they are better at gross motor skills earlier on. Play to their strengths by assigning them such jobs as carrying things to and from the table. You'll all be happier for it.

Setting the Table

The standard place setting in the United States is to position the napkin on the left with the fork on top, and the knife and spoon on the right with the knife inside the spoon. Drinks should be placed to the right above the knife and spoon; bread plates to the left above the napkin. That's standard, but it's okay to be flexible. Some families only use what they need on any given night—for soup and sandwiches, for example, the table setter might put out only spoons and extra napkins. This works very well for some families, but clearly has the potential for abuse—if your child sets the table with no utensils and suggests that in many countries, spaghetti is eaten with the fingers, don't buy it. On the other hand, if your kids are into the finer details of table setting, utensils are used from the outside moving in, so dessert forks would be placed closer to the plate than the dinner fork.

Give Thanks Where It's Due

When you have called everyone to the table, you may want to have your children wait for everyone to arrive before being seated. Whether you feel that is necessary for family meals is up to you, but it is a good habit to develop for restaurants and when you are a guest at another home. It shows a great deal of respect for the host. Many families offer some kind of blessing or grace before being seated, and saying thank you to the cook for dinner is a very nice gesture that makes the cook feel great. It also helps children recognize and appreciate the effort that has gone into the preparation of the meal, something that is generally taken for granted.

Just Say, "Yummmm" and Breathe Deeply

For many kids (and families) these days, life goes at a breakneck pace, and it's easy to rush through everything—including meals. As remarkable as it may seem, mealtimes can be soothing and even recharge your kids, regardless of their ages. Try to instill a "mealtime mindset," where everyone, including you, views mealtimes as more than just a quick refueling stop. Slow down, relax, and enjoy each other's company at the table. A 1996 study conducted by Harvard University's Graduate School of Education concluded that family dinners were more beneficial to child development than playtime, school, or storytime, so make the most of the time you spend eating together. Try to avoid or eliminate outside distractions so you can all focus on each other. While you may be tempted to use this time together to air grievances, avoid doing so if you can. Complaints and discipline can be discussed later, phone calls can be returned after you've eaten, television shows will re-run, and you may well find that you and your family reconnect at the dinner table.

Setting the Mood

After everyone is at the table and seated, they should take their napkins and put them on their laps (not on their heads like a scarf or over their hands like a magician). There should be no toys, books, or other distractions at the table, and the TV should be off. You'll find it's much easier for everyone to concentrate on eating and enjoying each other's company when they aren't mesmerized by something in another room. If you're a family who likes "mood music," you can offer the table setter the perk of being able to select some appropriate dinner music, subject to your approval, of course. You may not find Barney's Sing Along Songs or KOЯN the most conducive music to digestion—but then again, you might.

While it seems picky, encourage your children to sit up straight with their chairs pushed in and their elbows off the table, and the hand they aren't using to eat with in their laps. This will sound as difficult for some kids as patting their heads and rubbing their stomachs simultane- ously, but try to work on at least one of these skills at a time. It will help discourage your kids from tipping in their seats, or practically lying on the table, and having their hands in their laps rather than tapping on the table top or absently touch- ing everything near them will help avoid spills and ease your nerves and theirs.

Serving and Passing

No one should start eating until everyone is served and the hostess or host (or the starring helper—a huge perk) picks up his or her fork. If you have such a large group that food will get cold before everyone is served you can waive this rule for a given meal, but you should make your expectations clear. Generally speaking, it's not unreasonable to expect your children to wait the two minutes for everyone to be seated and served before digging in. If you have very young children who just can't wait, give them something like a cracker or a carrot to munch on while you or your helpers are serving the rest of the plates. This way they will still get the message that they must wait to start dinner until everyone is ready.

It's important to set some rules so that food passing doesn't degenerate into food football. A good general rule is that if someone asks for something to be passed, including condiments like ketchup, the person making the request gets it first, which means that as it heads  down the table it shouldn't be making pit stops at other people's plates on its way. You don't want it to be gone before it reaches its destination, or take so long to get there that it's no longer wanted—either scenario can cause serious dinnertime squabbles.

It's also important to teach your kids when it's okay to reach for something, and when they should ask for it to be passed. If whatever they want isn't directly in front of their plate and they can't reach it when their bottoms are squarely on the seat, they should go for the pass. Lunging across the table like an errant swordsman to reach anything is a definite no go.

GREAT DINNER!

Family Style vs. Restaurant Serving

Most families choose one of two ways to serve meals: family style or restaurant style. Family style meals are served at the table: all food is placed in dishes and brought to the table and everyone either serves themselves or is served by a designated person. At meals served restaurant style, on the other hand, food is placed on individual plates in the kitchen and brought to the table. Both methods have distinct advantages: family style serving means that the cook (most likely you) doesn't have to jump up and down from table to kitchen throughout the meal, while restaurant style serving creates a much less cluttered table, parental control over portion size and choice, and (usually) fewer spills.

You may find that a hybrid of the two styles works best: you serve plates with food on them for the first round, then put extras on the table for seconds.

Finish Firsts Before Going for Seconds

While eating, people should wait until everyone has been served "firsts" before asking for "seconds," and you can make a rule that to get seconds, the child has to eat all of everything else, even vegetables—before asking. This allows you or whoever else is doing the serving to eat at least part of the meal before serving all over again. It will also help you avoid having to give one of your kids the Heimlich maneuver because he gulped down his first serving of something everybody likes as quickly as possible so that he can be sure to get seconds before it is all gone.

You want a leisurely meal, not a race. It's also a nice idea for the person who takes the last of anything to say, "Mind if I take the rest of the French fries?" before she does. This helps avoid serious (and potentially loud) outbreaks of disappointment from other family members who may insist they weren't alerted that a dish was almost gone, and gives you the chance to divide the last serving more equally.

Remind them that the food isn't going to be taken away, and that it's not a contest to see how much they can eat, as fast as they can eat it.

If you're having something that you know your kids like to eat, remind them that the food isn't going to be taken away, and it's not a contest to see how much they can eat, as fast as they can eat it. Encourage them to take small-to-medium-sized, not mountainous, portions of food on their forks or spoons, and to bring the food to their mouths, not their mouths to their forks. If they can't easily fit into their mouths what is on their fork or spoon, they need to either cut it up or put some back.

Using Utensils

During meals, older children should eat with their utensils rather than their hands, unless you are serving finger foods—and you should be the judge of what constitutes a finger food. Kids three and under probably won't be able to manage keeping all of their food on their utensils without some help from their hands. Notice the effort they are making and reinforce it when you see it, because it's really hard to learn to use a utensil. Remember what it was like when you first tried using chopsticks? That's what it's like for your preschooler all the time.

While the youngest children can get away with holding their spoon or fork like a caveman as they are still working on their fine motor skills, remember that if your children can hold a crayon or pencil properly, you can expect them to hold a fork or spoon properly, as well.

The standard practice for cutting food is to hold the knife in the right hand and the fork in the left, bringing the knife blade across the back of the fork tines to cut, then switching the fork back to the right hand to take a bite. The continental style

Keep it Positive

It can be frustrating teaching your children manners—for both you and them—and there will undoubtedly be times when none of you is enjoying the lesson. Remember to try to keep your comments positive so that you spend most of your time teaching your kids what you want them to do, rather than reprimanding them for what they are doing wrong. Rather than saying, "Quit eating with your hands!" you could say, "Remember to use your fork, please." When you do see them exhibiting good manners, be sure to comment on it and reinforce it in a positive way. The more enthusiastically you praise their good habits, the more likely they are to retain them.

involves cutting the food in the same way, but keeping the fork in the left hand to eat. Either way is fine; the point is to teach your kids that they should actually use the utensils to eat with (not as weapons), rather than pretending they've never seen anything like them before.

Encourage them to practice cutting one piece of meat or whatever they are cutting at a time; there is no need to mince everything on their plate at once. Don't expect children younger than five or six to be able to use a knife with any dexterity, and many children will struggle with cutting until they are ten or older. So be patient, and flexible. You may want to avoid letting some children have a knife at their place altogether: many a tabletop sword fight can be avoided this way.

Talking at the Table

The great thing about having meals together is that it is an important time for family conversations. The difficult thing is that, especially for younger kids, it's hard for children to wait their turn to talk, even if they have mouths full of food. For some reason, kids find it hysterically funny to see other people talking with their mouths full. Adults don't. Sometimes kids talk at the same time they are chewing because they are worried they won't get their turn to tell you about their day. You can avoid this by telling your kids that you want to hear at least one thing that happened during their day and help them take turns—while one is relating his or her story, the others can be eating and listening.

Taking turns around the table is also a great way for children to get a chance in the spotlight, even for those who aren't necessarily big talkers or who have to compete with other siblings. Knowing they'll have a turn to talk, uninterrupted, often helps kids focus their thoughts, and you may learn things about their day or what's on their mind that you otherwise wouldn't have the opportunity to hear.

Younger kids, especially, want their turn to talk, but will often freeze when the time comes. Help them get started by keeping requests for conversation simple and specific, such as, "Noah, tell me something good (sad, upsetting, funny, silly, etc.) that happened to you today." Don't feel you have to avoid challenging, sad, or really funny topics at the table—these are the times when subjects of all kinds come up and the potential for rich and meaningful discussions and teaching-without-preaching moments for both you and your kids can happen.

When Good Talk Goes Bad

That said, you will need to set boundaries regarding conversations, especially those that involve funny incidents that get funnier and funnier as they are told and retold. Talking about things that are silly is as important as it is challenging, and you'll have to help your kids discover the fine line between dinner-table funny and out-of-control silliness. This includes other noises that can't be classified as actual words such as burps, farts, or other sounds. Make it clear what your expectations are—and what the consequences will be—if the conversation veers into the unacceptable, and be prepared to follow through if your kids aren't following your rules.

Bathroom talk stays in the bathroom.

Remember that most young kids aren't at a developmental age to fight the impulse to laugh if given any cue that it's okay, so model the behavior you want them to emulate. If someone accidentally burps or passes gas at the table, a quiet, "Excuse me" should suffice, and no one else should comment on it. If someone does, usually by laughing maniacally and making a huge deal of it, it's a good time to explain to the person reacting inappropriately that calling attention to it counts as bathroom talk, which is appropriate only in the bathroom. A suggestion to go there usually stops the giggles.

It is polite to wait until everyone is finished eating before leaving the table, although this might be unreasonable to expect of kids younger than four.

Finishing the Meal

Usually someone is a speed eater and will want to leave the table as soon as he or she is finished. It is polite to wait until everyone is finished eating before leaving the table, although this might be unreasonable to expect of kids younger than four. Even young children, however, should ask to be excused from the table, and you can expect them to bring their plates to the sink.

Cleaning Up

You can also expect your kids to help with mealtime clean up. Assign them specific tasks appropriate to their age. Older children can clear away dishes and help wash up, while younger ones can put back (unbreakable) condiments, pick up napkins, or push in chairs. The younger you start including your kids in participating in preparing and cleaning up meals, the more ingrained it will become. It takes a bit more time at the outset, but the results are worth it. And here's your chance to model good behavior for your kids by thanking them for their help, which also lets them know you appreciate their efforts.

Trying New Foods

While your children would probably prefer to eat the same thing night after night, you may not want to be trapped in pizza or chicken nuggets hell for the next ten or fifteen years. When you offer your children new or untried foods, be clear about what you expect from them in terms of eating it: some parents request that their children simply try new foods; others insists their children eat what they are given. You'll have to make that call for your family.

Whether your children like what you're serving or not, you can and should be tough about gagging noises, loud complaints, or negative comments about what they are eating. This definitely falls in the "if you don't have something nice to say, don't say anything at all" category. It is also good practice for when your children go out to eat at a restaurant or to a friend's house. Good manners travel well.

"No-Thank-You" Helpings

A good way to get your kids to try new foods or keep them trying ones they've arbitrarily decided they don't like, is to give them a "no-thank-you" helping option. No-thank-you helpings are tasting helpings, just big enough for a bite, and small enough that even the most finicky kid can finish. This often helps parents avoid food-related confrontations that don't benefit anyone. And in the end, if your child has a serious aversion to something and you know it, why set yourself up for something that is bound to fail? If you know that everyone in your family but you despises liver, and that to serve it is going to turn the dinner table into a liver-induced battleground, then make the wise choice and order it for yourself the next time you go out to eat.

Activities and Ideas for Reinforcing Good Table Manners

I Spy Good Manners
Age Range: 3–6

This is a good way to get everyone involved in both practicing and noticing good manners around them. Each time you or someone else at the table notices good manners being used by another person, you say, "I spy good manners. Sasha is using her fork instead of her fingers," and the person using good manners and the person noticing good manners both get a point. When someone reaches ten points, they get a small reward, such as choosing the next topic of conversation first.

Tea with the Queen
Age Range: 3–6

When your children sit down to a meal, announce that they are auditioning for an opportunity to go to tea with the Queen, and the children who have the best table manners will be invited. It's a good idea to give them only one or two points to focus on, such as holding their utensils properly. Little kids get a huge kick out of watching each other to see if anyone slips up, and they try very hard to "get invited." As a reward for their efforts, plan a quick tea party with real cups and saucers.

What Do You Say When . . .
Age Range: 3 and up

This is a fun way to help your kids internalize good manners and solve problems around the dinner table. You can take turns pre-senting somewhat outrageous table situations that your kids have to address. For example, you might say, "Billy is at his friend's house for dinner. He sits down to eat, and is served a big piece of squirrel brain. What should he do?" This game has the potential for lots of silliness, so you'll have to monitor it pretty carefully so it doesn't get out of control.

Finger Food Night
Age Range: 3 and up

With the help and planning of your kids, create an evening meal that is entirely made up of "finger food." This doesn't mean everyone just gets to eat dinner with their hands (some parents would wonder why that would be different from regular dinner); rather, allow each child to pick one or two dishes that are approved finger foods. Let them help you prepare the meal, and figure out how to set the table and what condiments or other implements you'll require. They'll love the opportunity to create a special meal like this, and you'll get them involved in the entire meal process.

Smorgasbord Buffet
Age Range: 3 and up

Here's another way to include your kids in meal preparation. While older kids may understand that this is really Leftover Night in disguise, your younger kids will think this is great—especially if you embellish it. Take out all of the leftovers you want to use up, and supplement it with small, special items that you let each child choose. It can be very simple, such as a slice of pizza cut up into bite-size pieces, jello, the last of the pickles—anything that's easy to serve. Put it all out on the table, buffet style, and let your kids choose what they want of each. You'll clean out your refrigerator, and your kids will think it's a special treat.

Talking Round Robin
Age Range: 3 and up

This is a good way to help your kids take turns talking about their day in a way that's not only polite, but also lets them be a part of the decision making process. You start by saying, "I'm going to tell you what my favorite part of today was," and when you're done, you pick out someone else and say, "Now Richard, you tell us what your favorite part of the day was, and then pick someone else." That child picks another, and so on, until everyone at the table has had at least one turn. It's surprising how politely kids will wait when they get to choose the next person in turn.

Table Setting Competition ✓
Age Range: 5 and up

This is a fun competition between two teams that will get your table set faster than you ever imagined. Have your kids split themselves up into teams on either side of the table. At your signal, they have to set half the table with "proper" place settings. Whoever does it the fastest and neatest wins the competition.

Dream Date with Mom or Dad
Age Range: 5 and up

For many children, especially those with more than one sibling, it's a real novelty to get out of the pack for one-on-one time with a parent. A lunch or dinner date is the perfect opportunity to share "quality time" and practice good manners with you and the restaurant staff. Let your child order for both of you, and help work out the bill and tip (if appropriate). You can also use this activity as a reward for exceptional table manners at home.

Extra Special Evening
All ages

Now and then look for reasons to have an extra special evening honoring a family member. Set the table with your best china, candles, a tablecloth—the works. Eat in the dining room if you have one. This is a good opportunity to enlist everyone's help in deciding what to serve, setting the table, serving the meal. A birthday is an obvious reason to hold a special dinner, but celebrating any kind of success, accomplishment, or milestone is a great way to make a child feel great. The formal setting and extra special preparations will encourage your children to be on their best behavior and use their best manners—and don't forget to make your high expectations clear before the meal. It will be good practice for the next time they go to Grandma's house for Thanksgiving.

Questions and Answers

Q. I have an eight-year old who consistently forgets to use good table manners—or he'll use some manners, and forget others. For example, he'll chew with his mouth closed and won't interrupt, but then he'll pick up food off his plate with his fingers. How can I help him remember to use good manners all the time?

A. *The best way to help your child use good manners all the time is by using positive reinforcement. Praise him for the manners that he is getting right, and remind him in a positive way about the behavior that isn't right. For example, if he's picking food up off his plate with his fingers, you could say, "Great job chewing with your mouth closed. Please remember to use your fork." Don't forget that there are a lot of distractions for an eight-year old at the table, and focusing on one or two skills a night will be more effective than constant reminders to correct many behaviors.*

Q. My kids are terrible about trying new foods, and they make eating at friends' houses almost impossible with their unwillingness to at least try what is served. How can I get them to be more open to trying new things for dinner?

A. *The best way to get kids excited about new things is to let them have a role in the process. Find some food magazines or cookbooks and let your kids help you plan a meal together, with the stipulation that it has to be something a bit different than usual. Maybe they've always wanted to try chopsticks, or have always wished they could eat a meal off Grandma's fancy china—incorporate some fun and excitement into the planning, and they will become invested and interested in the entire meal, from planning to cooking to eating. You may be surprised at the results. And once they've tried new foods successfully a few times, they may be more willing even when it's unexpected.*

Q. I love the dinner conversations we have, but occasionally the laughter and joking become almost too disruptive. What are some good guidelines about how much is too much fun at the table?

A. *Mealtimes are hugely valuable times for family communication, but as with most good group communication, family discussions usually require some kind of moderator. This will most likely be your role, and as the moderator you'll have the opportunity to model the kind of behavior you want your children to use. Clarify expectations—when you're asking them a question or turning the conversation from one topic or one person to another, say, "David, can you tell me in an indoor voice what was funny about your day?"*

This will also allow you to take a pro-active rather than a reactive approach to keeping the conversation at a level that encourages discussion without disruption—and should help you avoid getting to the point where you're yelling, "Stop laughing! There is too much fun going on here!"

Q. I feel like there are so many rules that my kids should learn about table manners that they—and I—will never figure them all out. Which ones are the really important ones and which ones can wait?

A. *The goal of this book is to outline most of what is considered standard "good" manners, not to point out everything you must do in order to be socially acceptable. You will need to decide what manners are important for you and your family, and help your children learn them to a level with which you're comfortable. Decide what would make mealtimes most enjoyable for all of you, and practice the manners that will help get you there. And don't try to conquer Rome in a day, or even a year. Good table manners are learned over time. It's a process.*

What to Expect

This section is divided into age groups that can be used as a quick reference for what you can and can't expect from your child in terms of table manners. You want to have high, but not unreasonable, expectations—otherwise success is sure to elude you. Please note that this is based on very general developmental milestones, and provides general guidelines for children—your child might be much more or less developmentally advanced, and therefore capable of more or less than indicated.

Also be aware that as children move toward the outer limits of the age ranges specified, they will be more likely to have a higher degree of proficiency at the skills listed.

From toddler to 24 months, you can expect your child to do the following:

- ✓ She will want to eat like other family members and will try to use utensils—give her a spoon for safety's sake.
- ✓ She will be a very messy eater.
- ✓ She'll drop food and utensils to practice cause and effect.
- ✓ She'll grunt and talk with her mouth full.
- ✓ As she approaches two, she'll increase her use of "no" and negotiating which foods she'll eat. You can help reinforce personal autonomy while still staying in control by offering an option: "Will you have peas or carrots?"
- ✓ She will be unable to sit through a long meal.
- ✓ She will watch you and others and learn from watching your table habits.

From 3 to 5 years, you can expect your child to do the following:

✓ He will be able to use a fork and spoon with more expertise, but will still spill.

✓ He will continue to talk with his mouth full and will need frequent reminders.

✓ He will have a short attention span but will notice and comment on how others are interacting.

✓ He may even let you know that others are breaking rules (5+) while not recognizing that he is as well.

✓ He can help set the table but will need many reminders— it is a good age to start with small, simple jobs.

✓ He will burp and make goofy sounds at the table and will need prompting to say "Excuse me." He also won't mean it when he says "Excuse me."

✓ He will likely interrupt conversations he is interested in.

✓ He may be ready for family restaurants at this age.

From 6 to 7 years, you can expect your child to do the following:

✓ She will have better motor control and should be able to use a knife while eating, but will still struggle with the knife and fork together.

✓ She will often eat with her mouth closed, but will still need reminders, especially when excited, such as at parties or in groups of people.

✓ She will be very "rules oriented" and will be able to recite your expectations at the table. "What are the rules? No talking with your mouth full, napkin on lap."

✓ She will be able to help set the table with fewer cues. For example, she'll be able to take the silverware to the table and place it around the plates.

✓ She will burp and make goofy sounds but will also say "Excuse me" on her own and with less prompting.

✓ She will occasionally interrupt but will be redirected more easily.

✓ She will be ready for family restaurants at this age.

From 8 to 10 years, you can expect your child to do the following:

✓ He will show increased skill setting the table.

✓ He will have a greater interest in the roles he plays: "I set the table, you clear the table."

✓ He will generally eat with his mouth closed and won't talk with his mouth full.

✓ His hand–eye coordination is more graceful, so his use of utensils is better.

✓ He will likely dine out with less boredom or the need to be quite so active, and fine restaurants are possible at this age.

From 11+ years, you can expect your child to do the following:

✓ She will be capable of achieving all the expectations laid out in Chapter 1, but may need reminders now and then, especially if over–excited or in a new situation.

WHAT DID YOU JUST SAY?

APPRoPRiate Language in eveRY SeHing

This could be you: you and your family are out at a restaurant. Everyone is behaving beautifully, the food is good, and the conversation is lively. A heavy-set woman and her husband at the table across the way are flirting with your three-year old, and everyone is having a great time. As the other couple gets up to leave, the woman stops by your table, bends down to your preschooler and says, "Hi there!" Your child looks at her and says, brightly "You're really fat!"

You fervently wish the floor would open up and swallow you, your preschooler, and the rest of your family immediately. But it doesn't. Instead, the woman gives you a nasty look, says, "Nice kid," and walks away, obviously very offended. You sit mortified, your preschooler is confused, and a distinct pall falls over the rest of the meal.

The Basics

This chapter will help you avoid situations like these, or deal with them when they inevitably occur. It covers topics ranging from learning how to give and receive compliments gracefully to how to talk respectfully about other people's differences. And while you may well experience that desperate, "swallow me whole right NOW" feeling again, with careful coaching and lots of patience, it will be a rarity.

Basic manners covered in this chapter:
* Saying please and thank you
* Learning to make and accept apologies
* Using an appropriate tone of voice
* Understanding which topics are appropriate for public conversations
* Interrupting
* Talking about differences
* Giving and accepting compliments

Please Note

This chapter deals with some of the Big Issues of raising children, including sex, money, and teaching tolerance. However, it does it strictly from the perspective of good manners: learning what's appropriate to say and when it's appropriate to say it. Please be aware that this chapter doesn't help you find ways to teach your kids about sex, offer the five steps to financial freedom, or tell your kids why some people are different, but it does help you teach them not to share their newfound knowledge at the neighbor's dinner table.

The Magic Words

Obviously the appropriateness of the language your children use will depend on the situation; your 13-year old isn't going to talk the same way to her best friends as she'd talk to her grandmother, and generally speaking, the older your children get, the better they'll be at assessing their audience and modifying their language accordingly.

There are, however, some key words and phrases that are important and appropriate all the time, regardless of age or situation. It's vital to teach your children the value of what many parents call "the magic words": please, thank you, and you're welcome. When your kids want something, they should say, "Please." When their request is granted, they should say, "Thank you," and when they are fulfilling a request and someone thanks them, they should say, "You're welcome."

It is never too early to teach your children that the way to get what they want is to use the magic words. Reinforce them every time your child makes a request, no matter how trivial it is, and you'll find that they become automatic. You may feel like you're nagging your kids—and you probably are—but insisting that they use these words is important, and the sooner they internalize them, the better. Simple good manners go a very long way, especially when your children are at someone else's home or in other social situations.

Excuse Me, Pardon Me, Beg Your Pardon

When your children are trying to get from point A to point B and there are obstacles in the way, they should use some variant of "Excuse me" rather than trying to force their way through as though it's the big game, and they need to make a touchdown. It's appropriate to say "Excuse me" to others whenever you cross their personal space—whether it's by scooting close by, crossing or reaching in front, burping or passing gas in their presence, or actually touching or bumping them. Learning about personal space can be difficult for younger kids—as far as they are concerned, every space is their personal space. Help your children become aware of other people and where your children are in relation to them, so they can recognize when they are crossing into someone else's space. Most people are perfectly willing to share their space briefly when alerted, and your kids will find it easier to negotiate their way, as well.

Learning to Apologize

There are few things more difficult for children than apologies—both giving them and accepting them gracefully. However, it's important to do so. Whether there's a misunderstanding over who ate the last Pop Tart, or a friend dropped the LEGO ship your son just made, an apology made and accepted brings closure to the incident—whether the incident was accidental or deliberate—and helps wipe the slate clean.

A proper apology requires very little: whether he is feeling especially sorry or not, your child should look at the person to whom he is apologizing in the eye, and say a simple, "I'm sorry," in a tone that sounds somewhat sincere—there's no point apologizing if the tone itself is an invitation to Round 2.

Accepting an apology gracefully is as important as making one. The child receiving an apology should acknowledge the gesture being made with some verbal answer, such as, "That's okay," or "Apology accepted." Even if the aggrieved party isn't feeling very forgiving, she should accept the apology that is extended, remembering that the next time she may be on the apologizing end. What she shouldn't do is rub it in—help your children learn that once an apology has been made and accepted, the incident is over. It isn't appropriate and certainly doesn't help a sensitive situation when one friend apologizes to another, and the second one says, "That's okay, but it really WAS your fault, you know." Be prepared to practice this over and over and over and over . . .

Because it's not easy to turn off hurt feelings, you may want to enforce a "two-minute time-out" rule, similar to a hockey penalty box, where the aggrieved parties go to neutral corners to cool off before resuming play.

It isn't appropriate and certainly doesn't help a sensitive situation when one friend apologizes to another, and the second one says, "That's okay, but it really WAS your fault, you know."

Tone of Voice

Teaching your kids to use good manners when they are speaking isn't just a matter of what they say; it's also how they say it. Any parent who has been told, "Whatever," by their prepubescent child in a tone that a Valley Girl would be proud of understands the issue.

Small children, especially, seem to have to only two volumes: loud and off.

For younger kids, it's generally a volume control problem. Small children, especially, seem to have only two volumes: loud and off. A good way to teach your youngest children about what tone is appropriate in different situations is to help her understand the difference between indoor and outdoor voices, and refer to them as such. Take your child outside and allow her to make as much noise as possible (or as much as you and your neighbors can stand), and explain that this is an outdoor voice. Then bring her inside and model the tone and volume appropriate for inside your household. Let her practice both indoor and outdoor voices in their respective environments, and continue to refer to them as "indoor" and "outdoor" voices when she needs a reminder. See page 51 for more ideas to reinforce "indoor" and "outdoor" voices. Older kids also often need a reminder, and saying, "Indoor voices, please," is a much kinder, gentler way to ask than yelling, "Quiet!"

Older kids also often need a reminder, and saying, "Indoor voices, please," is a much kinder, gentler way to ask than yelling,
"Quiet!"

For older children, volume can be less of a problem than the tone in which they say things. Generally this becomes an issue when your kids are sulky, crabby, asked to do something they don't want to do, or simply exercising their right to irritate you. You will have to make the call regarding what tone of voice is acceptable and what isn't, and what the consequences should be. Conversations between adults and children should be based on an established level of trust and respect on both sides, but it's important to remember that it isn't an equal level—as the parent, you'll have to make sure that the balance of respect is tipped in your favor. Kids who learn to speak respectfully to adults are kids adults like to be around, and your children will need to learn that the tone they use to speak to adults, no matter what their mood or circumstance, affects the way adults treat them in return. See "Don't Use That Tone With Me!" on page 52 for a fun way to show your kids how their tone of voice affects others.

Bathroom Talk Stays in the Bathroom

Bathroom talk is usually an issue for younger children. For some reason, bathroom talk is the favorite conversational topic among young boys— they can spend hours discussing and laughing hysterically over their bodily functions. And it's contagious, so beware—even the most perfectly behaved children succumb when they are around bathroom talkers, and the more you protest, the funnier it gets.

Kids are curious about, and need to discuss, how their bodies work, and it's natural and healthy to do so. In the bathroom. Allow your kids to ask questions, be silly, and talk bathroom talk in the bathroom and you'll probably find that they don't bring it up at the table or other inappropriate places. And if they do, a reminder that, "Bathroom talk stays in the bathroom," with an invitation to go there to discuss it is often enough.

Talking About Money

There's nothing like overhearing a conversation between two children as they discuss their parents' net worth, usually in disappointed tones, in public. Some adults are comfortable discussing their personal finances with, or in front of, their children, but many aren't. Talking excessively about money and what things cost is considered bad manners. This extends to discussing how much gifts cost, asking people if they are rich and how they got that way, and wondering aloud how much money their parents' friends make, usually in front of said parents.

There is a difference between teaching your children about the value of money, which is obviously very important and necessary (they won't fall for the, "but the nickel is BIGGER than the dime" trick for very long), and teaching them to value things based on their unit cost.

Explain to your children that talking a lot about money makes many people very uncomfortable, and to make someone feel that way isn't polite. Let them know that most adults consider their finances both personal and private, and do not welcome comments or questions related to them. In addition, most kids don't

have an accurate idea of their family's finances and consequently get it all wrong. Your children will certainly have questions about other people's—and your own—money, and you'll have to decide how much information to give them. It's always a good idea to stress to children that gifts are valuable because of the intentions of the giver, and that people like to hear positive comments about their houses or other nice things they own, but discussions over how much they cost or how people can afford them are best left to more private conversations with you.

Talking About Sex

Usually children become interested in talking about sex when they begin elementary school . . .

Sex is another topic that makes many adults uncomfortable when kids start discussing it. Usually children become interested in talking about sex when they begin elementary school: they are just old enough to hear or see references to it, and too young to be embarrassed by it. Generally, conversations young children have about sex involve copious amounts of misinformation, usually attributed to another child who knows a lot about all sorts of stuff that you wish he didn't.

How you tackle talking to your children about sex is obviously up to you; however, as a matter of etiquette, when the subject does come up you can explain to your children that sex is private, and talking about sex is also for private conversations with you rather than as a new and interesting topic of discussion during carpool or dinner at Jimmy's house.

Giving Compliments

Learning to give compliments is primarily a matter of voicing the nice things you're thinking about another person while the other person is around to hear them. Encourage your kids to put into words the nice things they are thinking about others, especially when the thought is appreciative—giving a simple compliment such as, "This dinner is great," or "You look nice," can make a huge difference to the person doing the work or making the effort. The one rule for giving compliments is that they should be sincere: giving compliments based on an ulterior motive is usually not only very obvious to the recipient but also calls into question sincere compliments the person may give at other times. You can also let your kids know that however desperate you are for appreciation, "Mom, you aren't THAT old looking" isn't really a compliment.

Just Say Thanks

The best, and most polite response to a compliment is a simple, "Thank you."

For many people, accepting compliments can be more difficult than giving them. Compliments draw attention to something a person has done or said, and as children become more aware of their place in the world, the idea that others notice what they do can be both exciting and disconcerting. A natural tendency, especially for girls as they get older and more self-conscious, is to deflect compliments away from themselves, explaining what isn't good about what they've done, or why they don't look lovely. Teach your children, and especially your daughters, that a compliment is given as a gift, and should be accepted as a gift. The best, and most polite response to that gift is a simple, "Thank you."

Interrupting

It's hard to take turns talking when you have a great idea. It's even harder not to get upset at someone else when they butt in on what you're saying. Interrupting is one of the biggest causes of kid squabbles, and no wonder—it's unbelievably irritating to be cut off or talked over when you have something important to say. As parent and general referee of all things unfair in your family, you'll have to help your children take turns talking without being interrupted. It's a good idea to have a general "one person at a time" policy, where one child gets the floor for a limited amount of time with no interruptions, and then answers questions from other family members about the topic before another child gets center stage. Another option is to create a loose rotation of who gets to talk first so that children waiting know that the next time it will be their turn to go first. This may help you avoid the "but I'm not done telling you about my dream" wail from the child in the spotlight, when others waiting try to interject their own comments or stories. Teaching your kids to take turns talking and to wait politely and patiently is a lesson that will serve them well later in life, and one that they'll undoubtedly have to practice. See page 32, in Chapter 1, for more ideas about taking turns during conversations.

Swears Really Stick

Beware the swear! Toddlers parrot the world around them, regardless of the delicacy of the language. So when you drop that jar on your foot or hammer your thumb, bite your tongue before belting out a couple of choice words, or you may hear your adorable three-year old saying, "Daddy, look at that #!&@ flower!"*

Talking About Differences

Back at that restaurant where your preschooler called someone fat, how could you have avoided that situation? The fact is, you probably couldn't. Your three-year old noticed something about the woman at the next table, and talked about it. From his perspective, it was no different than noticing that the napkins were paper or the booth was red naugahyde. That's one of the things that is so amazing and wonderful about kids: they experience the world with a judgment-free perspective. To them, the norm is what they live with, and anything other than that is something to take notice of, comment on, and store away for future reference. It's your job as a parent to help your children talk about the differences they recognize between themselves and other people in a manner that's socially appropriate.

Encourage your young kids to talk with you about how people are different . . .

Encourage your young kids to talk with you about how people are different, but also explain to them that other people are aware of the differences, too, and don't need your child to point them out to them in great detail. And if your child inadvertently insults someone else because she notices differences that don't need to be voiced, it's appropriate and kind to apologize on her behalf.

It's also important to teach your children to respect the differences they can't see, and the best way to do this is model the behavior you want your kids to use. Think carefully before you tell an ethnic joke, or make jokes or comments about religion, race, gender, or sexual orientation, however benign they may seem to you. Teaching tolerance to your children means being tolerant yourself.

Activities and Ideas for Reinforcing Good Manners While Speaking

Headline News
Age Range: 3 and up

This game helps your kids take turns speaking, and also helps keep every child interested in the conversation, even if it isn't about them. When one child has big news to report—whether it's the lead in the school play, the fact that he did well on a test, or that she stayed dry all day—he or she should go first to report. Usually you'll find one event seems "bigger" than others, so that person can go first. Being the first to give headline news is also a reward that your kids will come to appreciate and want to strive for.

"Indoor and Outdoor Voices"
Age Range: 4 and under

This game helps younger kids realize what is an appropriate volume for speaking inside the house. You tell your children you will give them a character to play (an animal works well) and say either, "Indoor" or "Outdoor." They then act like that character, modulating their volume to match your instruction. For example, you'd say, "Okay, Chris. You're a lion. Outdoor voice. Now indoor voice." And the child will roar or growl accordingly.

Compliment Game
Age Range: 4 and up

The best way to learn to give and receive compliments is to practice doing it. This is a good game to do in the car, at the table, or any place where your family or children are gathered. You start by giving the person next to you a compliment; it can be as simple as saying, "Noah, you have a very nice smile." Noah should then thank you, and turn to the person next to him and give that person a compliment, and so on down the line. Bonus: your children say and hear nice things about each other.

"Don't Use That Tone With Me!"
Age Range: 4 and up

This activity can be a lot of fun, especially for budding dramatists. Present a scenario that is subjective enough so that a person's tone can make a big difference in interpretation—for example, someone's reaction to another person tripping and falling with a bag of groceries. Then either assign or let your kids choose roles to play: surly, sympathetic, angry, as mean as possible, as kind as possible, etc., and have them act out the scene. Games like this usually work best—and are more fun—when you are in the car or at home so your kids aren't intimidated or embarrassed by people watching them play another role.

 ## *A Walk in Their Shoes*
Age Range: 5 and up

A good way to teach younger children about respect and tolerance of other people is to encourage them to "take a walk in someone else's shoes." Have them mentally switch places with someone else and ask them questions based on their own behavior. Do they want other people to stare at them? Do they need another person to tell them what's different about them or do they already know? What do they want other people to notice about them? This is a game that kids play very well, and you may be surprised at the sophisticated and thoughtful responses they give when they are walking in someone else's shoes.

Put Your Money Where Your Mouth Is
Age Range: 5 and up

This will help you model the behavior you expect, in this case to control swearing, as well as to reinforce to your kids that there are many words that are never acceptable. Decide what words you consider to be swears, and any other words you don't want your kids using on a regular basis ("shut up" or "you idiot," for example). You don't have to list the worst swears you know, but you need to make clear what words and phrases are unacceptable. If your kids catch you saying one of these words you have to pay a penalty, like a quarter, five pushups, or no dessert. The same goes if you catch them. Your kids will love it when you slip up, and when they do, at least they'll pay for it!

Questions and Answers

Q. My neighbor's kids come over to our house often, and they never say please or thank you. It drives me nuts. What's a good way to address it with them?

A. *You can tell them very nicely that at your house, your rules apply, and if they want something, they should say please and thank you. If you want to be more subtle you can prompt them when the situation presents itself with a simple "What do you say?" or "What's the magic word?" Also remember to reinforce it when you hear it. A simple comment such as, "Thanks for using such good manners" is fine.*

Q. I have a toddler who uses bathroom talk all the time—he thinks it's outrageously funny, and I can even hear him muttering it to himself as he plays. Should I ignore it or reprimand him every time he uses it? The other kids find it hysterical and I'm sure that's part of the problem.

A. *Toddlers and preschoolers use bathroom talk a lot—and it's understandable, considering that the transition from diapers to toilet training is looming large in their lives. Toddlers talk out their learning process, which is both normal and necessary, but you can and should set limits on where it's appropriate, which is in the bathroom or in private. Take him to the bathroom when he feels the need to use bathroom talk. You'll need to remind him without punishing him, and redirect him to something else immediately afterward.*

Q. My preschooler gets very upset when adults talk to him and smile at him in public. He often yells, "Stop staring at me!," or "I wasn't talking to you!" at them, which is very embarrassing. What's the best way to address this?

A. *Kids at this age are often very self conscious and have anxiety about their self image. Talk it through with him and explain that other people find him "handsome" or "nice" and may look at him because he is liked. Put your arm around him for reassurance to refocus his concern at being watched as a positive thing and ask him to give a simple smile back at the adult.*

Q. My 14-year old daughter has friends who swear a lot. They don't do it much when they know I'm around, but I can hear them (including my daughter) cuss up a storm when I'm not in the room. I don't like hearing such lovely girls talk like that, but I also don't want to embarrass my daughter in front of her friends. What can I do about this?

A. *Talk to your daughter alone first and point out that you are aware of her behavior when she is with her peers. Clarify your rules regarding swearing and warn her that the next time you hear them swearing you will interrupt. Don't be apprehensive about parenting your daughter. Parenting is about respect and understanding and not about being a friend. Through your earned respect, you will enjoy a peer-like relationship when she is an adult.*

What to Expect

This section is divided into age groups that can be used as a quick reference for what you can and can't expect from your child in terms of appropriate language in a variety of settings. You want to have high, but not unreasonable, expectations—otherwise success is sure to elude you. Please note that this is based on very general developmental milestones, and provides general guidelines for children—your child might be much more or less developmentally advanced, and therefore capable of more or less than indicated.

Also be aware that as children move toward the outer limits of the age ranges specified, they will be more likely to have a higher degree of proficiency at the skills listed.

From toddler to 24 months, you can expect your child to do the following:

✓ She will parrot almost everything she hears—so watch what you say and model what you want to hear from her!

✓ She will echo "Thank you" (and any other words) if you model it for her, but she will not mean it, and is not likely to say "Sorry" spontaneously.

✓ She will likely use bathroom talk as she moves through toilet training. She needs to talk out the process and should have a place to do so (like in the bathroom, not at the table).

From 3 to 5 years, you can expect your child to do the following:

✓ He will say words such as "Sorry," "Please," "Thank you," and "Excuse me" with prompting, but he will not mean it when he says them.

✓ He will need to be reminded regularly to use an "indoor voice" and "gentle touch."

✓ He will focus on potty humor at around 5+ (boys will especially do this), and you'll need to stress the difference between playground talk and family talk.

From 6 to 7 years, you can expect your child to do the following:

✓ She will say, "Sorry," "Please," "Thank you," and "Excuse me," etc., with meaning, and can generate these words herself at times.

✓ She will show signs of empathy for others, including pets.

✓ She will regress when she's in groups of other kids, and will need to have expectations for behavior stressed before and during group time.

✓ She will interrupt to keep from forgetting her thought or idea, especially when she's excited about the discussion.

✓ She may burp or make other noises for laughs, and should be reminded to say, "Excuse me."

From 8 to 10 years, you can expect your child to do the following:

✓ He will understand right and wrong in different situations.

✓ He will need less prompting and modeling here if you've been consistently doing both at earlier ages.

✓ He will pride himself on his self reliance and mastery of rules. Join with him in noticing how he follows the rules on his own and how proud you are of his doing so.

From 11+ years you can expect your child to do the following:

✓ She will have internalized and mastered the language skills explained in this chapter.

✓ She will respond well to positive feedback about her interactions with others, including adults. (Remember that boys may be more doers than talkers at this age, so notice and comment positively on their actions.)

I'd Like You to Meet...

Meeting and Greeting Adults & Others

Picture this: you're walking down the street with your teenage niece and your eight-year old, and you bump into someone you haven't seen in years. When you make introductions your niece steps up, extends her hand, and says, "Hi, I'm Elizabeth. It's nice to meet you." You are thoroughly impressed and proud to be her relative. Meanwhile, your eight-year old has stepped in gum and is too absorbed investigating various methods of removal to look up and acknowledge the visitor's presence. Later, as you look back on the incident and chisel hardened Hubba Bubba off your son's clothes, you marvel at your niece's good manners and vow to yourself that the next time you run into an old friend, your child will also be a meeting and greeting star. This chapter will help you get there. It covers the basics of introductions, greetings, and general good manners when the worlds of adults and children, acquaintances and strangers, collide.

The Basics

One of the most important things to remember when you're trying to teach your children how to introduce themselves, or be introduced, to adults is that for most children, adults are pretty intimidating creatures—they are not only physically much larger, but they represent unknown and unfamiliar social territory. Some kids are born hams and love the extra attention that talking with adults provides (those kids, in fact, are the kind that you often can't shut up when you're ready to move on), but most view chance meetings with adults as roadblocks on the way to somewhere more fun. The best way to help your kids learn good meeting and greeting skills is consistently to model the behavior you want them to exhibit, keep the interactions to a reasonable length (from a kid's perspective), and not push it when they are tired, hungry, or both—or you'll deeply regret it.

Basic meeting and greeting manners covered in this chapter:

* Acknowledging the presence of others
* Shaking hands
* Making eye contact
* Answering the door
* Taking part in adult conversations
* Entering and leaving a room

Take it Slowly

If your children are younger or very shy, don't force them to shake hands. Saying "Hi" or just making eye contact will do. It's better to start slowly and get your kids comfortable with the process of introductions than to force them to do things they aren't ready to do.

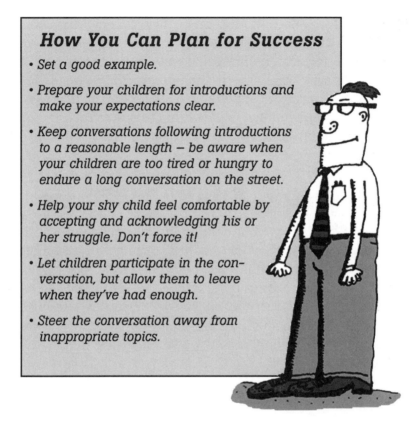

How You Can Plan for Success

- *Set a good example.*

- *Prepare your children for introductions and make your expectations clear.*

- *Keep conversations following introductions to a reasonable length – be aware when your children are too tired or hungry to endure a long conversation on the street.*

- *Help your shy child feel comfortable by accepting and acknowledging his or her struggle. Don't force it!*

- *Let children participate in the conversation, but allow them to leave when they've had enough.*

- *Steer the conversation away from inappropriate topics.*

Prepare Them for Introductions

When your kids are meeting another adult for the first time, try to ease the way by preparing them for it and leading them through it. Tell them what to expect from the adult they'll be meeting, and what you expect them to do in return. For example, "Here comes Mrs. Jones. She'll want to hug you. If you prefer not to be hugged, hold out your hand for a handshake, and say, 'Nice to meet you,' or 'Hi.'" That way, when Mrs. Jones comes up ready to hug your daughter, she'll know that she can stick out her hand in response instead, and still be perfectly polite.

The general rule for introductions is that younger people are introduced to older people; therefore, if you are introducing your daughter to an adult friend, you'd say, "Susie, this is Mrs. Jones." She should look Mrs. Jones in the eye, shake her hand (younger children may not feel comfortable shaking hands) and say, "Nice to meet you" or even just "Hi." When the conversation is over, your child should acknowledge that as well, and a simple, "Bye" is fine.

Addressing Adults by Name

Be sure to be clear to your children about how you want them to address the person they are meeting. Usually, the relationships you have with other adults will determine how your kids should address them; for example, if everyone in your town refers to each other by their first names, you will probably introduce your children to adults using their first names. If you're not sure how your adult friends want to be introduced, just ask them and act accordingly.

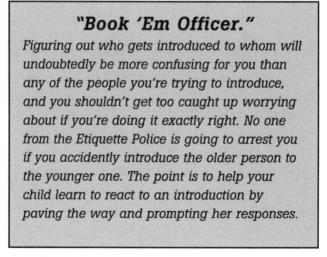

"Book 'Em Officer."
Figuring out who gets introduced to whom will undoubtedly be more confusing for you than any of the people you're trying to introduce, and you shouldn't get too caught up worrying about if you're doing it exactly right. No one from the Etiquette Police is going to arrest you if you accidently introduce the older person to the younger one. The point is to help your child learn to react to an introduction by paving the way and prompting her responses.

If you don't know the person very well and you're not comfortable asking him what his preference is, it's always better to lean toward the formal rather than the informal and use the adult's surname: Mr. Jones, Ms. Parker, etc. It is a sign of respect, and many adults, especially older ones, will expect it as a matter of courtesy. If the adults want your child to call them by their first names, they will let your child know.

Remember also that the way you refer to people in their absence may be the way your child remembers and refers to them. Be careful with nicknames for people you know whom your children may meet, especially those that are less than flattering; if you don't want your four-year old calling Mrs. Jones "that old wombat" to her face, don't call her that behind her back.

Hugs and air kisses: what to do

In some social circles, the handshake has been replaced by the hug or the air kiss, especially among people you know well. If you are comfortable with these forms of greeting and practice them yourself, your children may be receptive to them, too. However, many children are not comfortable being hugged and kissed by people they don't know well—which is understandable, considering how often they've been told that adults they don't know shouldn't be hugging and kissing them. If you face a social occasion where this may happen, let your children know they are allowed to respond in a way that's comfortable for them. If they don't want to be hugged or kissed, a handshake or even a hands-off "Hi" is fine. You can pick up your younger children if they need protection from an unwanted hug.

Make Eye Contact

It's important for kids to look adults in the eye when they are introduced and when they are speaking to them. It's also important to speak clearly. This can be difficult for some children, especially those who tend to be shy. It is intimidating to talk to adults, more so when they are unfamiliar. You can make this easier by keeping the interaction between your child and the adult short, and by telling your child exactly what you expect from her. You'll certainly have to practice at home. Sometimes kids, especially younger ones, don't get the "eye is a window to the soul" concept, and think that if they turn their face toward you, you can't tell that their eyes are still glued to the puppy across the street. Prompt your kids to make eye contact with you at home when they are speaking to you, and be as specific as possible. Rather than say, "Pay attention when I'm talking to you," say, "Look at my eyes when we talk together." A fun way to practice this is to have contests to see who can hold eye contact the longest while you are conversing, without looking at something else. (See "Eye Contact Contest" on page 67)

Answering the Door

Learning to open the door to greet guests politely is a very basic and important skill, but it's one that parents really can't take for granted any more.

When you are teaching your young children how to answer the door, you'll need to make it clear to them that they should never open the door to people they don't know. The best way to reinforce this in a positive way is to role play different scenarios as much as possible (See "Who's at

62

the Door" on page 66). Not only is it okay, it's very important not to be welcoming when a stranger is at the door. Follow up your game with a serious discussion about safety around strangers.

When you feel your children are old enough to answer the door to people they know, they should open the door and greet the visitor by name, and welcome the guest in. Older children should offer to take the guests' coats, bags, and other belongings, and then escort them to the place you usually receive guests. Practice this and have a plan for where your kids should put guests' things when they arrive—it's disconcerting to leave someone's house and find your dress coat dumped on the back hall floor.

Helping Shy Kids With Introductions

You will need to be patient with your shy child when helping her learn to interact socially with adults or new people, but you shouldn't let her get away without participating at all. Often breaking a social interaction down into a concrete, step-by-step script helps shy kids learn and become more comfortable with what to expect from the interaction. Practicing and role playing with your child in a safe and comfortable setting will go a long way to making her more comfortable to get through it one step at a time, and it's very important not to show anger or embarrassment when your shy child struggles. It's worth the effort. You can also make a habit of drawing your child close to you when greeting an adult so she feels more secure.

Entering the Room

When an adult enters your home, everyone—not just the kids—should stand up and acknowledge their arrival. If the person is someone the child knows well, a quick "Hi" is sufficient. If the adult in the room is a new acquaintance, the same protocol for introductions applies to meeting adults in your own home as it does on the street.

It should be a common understanding or house rule that when your guests come over, adults have precedence in public places in your home. That means if your kids are playing video games or watching movies in the place you'll be receiving visitors, they must concede the space to you. You shouldn't have to talk over or around other activity, and unless your children are very small and need immediate supervision, they should either be participating socially with you and your guests or excuse themselves to go else-where. The best way to do this without causing a serious uproar is to warn your children well before the visit is to take place. No one likes to be disturbed in the middle of the best part of the movie or during the trickiest level of a game, and starting out a visit by wit-nessing an enormous family fight is awkward for everyone.

GOLDEN RULE

The Golden Rule:
Acknowledge the presence of others.

Perhaps the most important social skill children should learn regarding meeting or greeting other people is to acknowledge the presence of others, whether they walk into a room or meet them on the street. Even the shyest child can and should learn to look the person in the eye, and either shake hands, say "Hi," or wave.

Remember Your Audience

Remember your audience and keep conversations short and appropriate for the age of your children. It can be excruciating for children, regardless of their age, to endure the long conversations that sometimes follow introductions. Younger children will likely not want to be included in the conversation; they'll just want it to end so they can get back to doing whatever they were engaged in before they were so inconveniently interrupted. On the other hand, no child likes to be ignored entirely, and will most likely make you pay dearly if you do. Allow your children the opportunity to take part in the conversation if they choose to; also make it clear to them when it's acceptable to take their leave of the conversation. Remind them to say "Excuse me" or a simple "Bye" as they go, as a way of closing out their participation.

It can be excruciating for children, regardless of their age, to endure the long conversations that sometimes follow introductions.

Older children can and should be included in the conversations that follow introductions so they don't feel awkward. It will help them to practice speaking without mumbling and to look directly at their audience, providing them an opportunity to practice being a "grown up." Try to give your child a chance to talk about something that interests him. Remember that most kids, even older ones, respond best to concrete questions relevant to their own experiences. If your 13-year old can talk about his favorite music group, or what his favorite sport is and why he likes it, he'll have the chance to participate willingly and well. In general, when including older children and teenagers in your conversations, remember the topic and language should always be appropriate; if it isn't, steer either the child or the subject somewhere else.

Activities and Ideas for Reinforcing Good Manners When Greeting Others

✿ *The Handshake Game*
Age Range: 3 and up

The simple act of looking someone in the eye, shaking hands and saying "Hello, it's nice to meet you" (nice to see you) or "Goodbye, it was nice to meet you" (see you) takes lots of practice. Make a game of it now and then—when seeing your children off or greeting them after they've been out, stick out your hand, look your child in the eye and say, "It's good to see you," or "Hello, how are you Sam?" or something like that. Kids love this game and it will help them memorize the whole process so it becomes automatic. It also will help your child feel comfortable with this social custom.

"Who's at the Door?"
Age Range: 3–6

This game will help reinforce to your children when it is appropriate for them to open the door. Children stand on one side of the door, you stand on the other. You knock, your child says, "Who is it?" and you either name a person familiar to them, or someone they won't know. Kids should then either open the door and greet their guest, or say, "I don't know you so I can't let you in. I'll go get my mother." You will tire of this game MUCH sooner than your little ones will—for some reason, younger kids find this game riotously funny.

Eye Contact Contest
Age Range: 4 and up

Break out the Visine. This contest helps your children make and keep eye contact while they are speaking, and it's fun to boot. At your signal, partners have a conversation about a topic you have chosen and must keep their eyes fixed on the other person's at all times, regardless of the distractions around them. The other person can try to distract his partner but cannot use his hands to do so. Blinking is allowed.

Queen or King for a Day
Age Range: 4–8

This game has a double benefit: you'll be helping your children learn good manners and you finally get to be treated like the Queen or King. Announce to your children that His or Her Royal Highness is visiting, and have them practice all of the meeting and greeting skills discussed in this chapter with you acting as royalty. It's also fun to surprise one child at a time with an unexpected chance to be a Crown Prince or Princess.

"Who Am I?"
Age Range: 5–8

This is a three-person game that helps children learn to be comfortable with introductions and short conversations with adults. One child can play the older adult, the other will be introduced to the "adult" by you. You assign the "adult" a career or unique personality that the younger child needs to guess through clues given during their (polite) introductory conversation, facilitated by you. This game prepares children surprisingly well for "real" conversations with older adults. Examples:

✓ Doctor   ✓ Chef

✓ Ballet Dancer   ✓ Garbage Collector

🌸 *Finding Common Ground*
Age Range: 8 and up

Most children are perfectly capable of carrying on intelligent, interesting conversations with adults—if they are given a topic that interests them or is concrete and experiential enough for them to relate to. To avoid grunts and mumbles when your kids are introduced to other adults, give them something to talk about: prepare them by finding something they will have in common with or find interesting about the adult they are meeting, and keep it as concrete as possible. For example, if you know that the friend you are introducing to your child is a doctor and your child is interested in biology, mention the common interest for them to use as a jumping off point for conversation.

Double Team 🌸
Age Range: teenagers

Often teenagers find safety—and poise—in numbers. If you're having guests and want to include your teenagers in the social interaction, allow them to have a trusted friend join them. It will provide your teenager with moral support and confidence, which usually translates into a much nicer social interaction for everyone—and provides valuable practice time for interacting with adults in a social situation.

Questions and Answers

Q. I have a teenager who isn't necessarily shy, but who doesn't do well interacting with adults once he's been introduced to them. He just grunts or mumbles and looks at the ground when they ask him a question, and it's very obvious that he isn't interested in the conversation. It's embarrassing for me and uncomfortable for the other adults, although it doesn't seem to bother him. What do I do?

A. *Help your son by creating opportunities to introduce him to other adults, and providing them with concrete cues to use for conversation starters. For example, if he's interested in mountain biking, introduce him with, "This is my son, Elisha. He's just back from a long mountain bike ride." Then the adult to whom you are introducing him can ask specific questions about something your son is interested in, is concrete, and very experiential, and will give him some safe and familiar ground to use as conversation. Also remember that for most teenagers, the contact they have with adults is generally pretty one-sided: adults talk and they endure it. Let him try out his conversation skills for short periods of time and give him an out soon after the introduction. But don't give up. He just needs practice, and help from you with the conversation.*

Q. An elderly male friend of the family is in the habit of kissing and hugging my children whenever he sees them. It was fine when they were younger, but my 13-year-old daughter, especially, is now uncomfortable. Any suggestions on how to address it?

A. *Do not allow your daughter to endure kisses and hugs she doesn't want to receive. If she is uncomfortable being hugged by this person when she greets him, she can extend her hand for a warm handshake and give a verbal greeting. You can support her by keeping an arm around her when this takes place so that she isn't drawn into a hug she doesn't want. Remember that you are her protector: it is your responsibility to keep your daughter safe and secure, so take the friend aside and explain (out of your daughter's presence) that she isn't comfortable with his hugs anymore—part of growing up—and she'd rather he didn't do it.*

Q. My sons, 7 and 9, often forget what they are supposed to do when meeting adults, and I find myself coaching them through it every time. Is this okay, or do I just let it go and talk to them about it later and hope they'll remember next time?

A. *Good manners are good habits, and they need to be practiced. It's fine and helpful to coach your kids gently about what to do during a social interaction, especially if your sons seem to be floundering. It's an even better idea to prepare them for what is about to happen, immediately before you greet the adults, so their mission is clear and fresh in their minds.*

Q. At what age should I start introducing my children to adults? I have a three-year old and a two-year old, and I feel kind of foolish making proper introductions to them.

A. *The earlier you model the behavior you want your children to exhibit, the sooner they will. Very young children are just as interested in the people around them as older kids, and it's a great idea to help them put familiar names and faces together. Remember to keep the introductions short and to the point, and if the kids aren't interested in interacting, or are too tired and hungry, move on. They are too young to control impulses or their tempers for very long. If you can make these encounters positive and successful at an early age, it will pay off as they mature.*

What to Expect

This section is divided into age groups that can be used as a quick reference for what you can and can't expect from your child in terms of interacting with others for the first time. You want to have high, but not unreasonable, expectations—otherwise success is sure to elude you. Please note that this is based on very general developmental milestones, and provides general guidelines for children—your child might be much more or less developmentally advanced, and therefore capable of more or less than indicated.

Also be aware that as children move toward the outer limits of the age ranges specified, they will be more likely to have a higher degree of proficiency at the skills listed.

From toddler to 24 months, you can expect your child to do the following:

✓ He will enjoy interactions with others provided a close family member or primary care giver is close by.

✓ He will be able to enjoy parallel play and cooperative interactions with other children, although he will not actually play with other kids.

✓ He will be very curious and watch others.

✓ He may tolerate being greeted by and having his hand shaken by unfamiliar adults.

✓ He will learn a sense of self worth by being acknowledged by adults, so definitely introduce him when you greet others.

From 3 to 5 years, you can expect your child to do the following:

✓ She will say "Hi" or "Hello" on her own (usually by 4+).

✓ She will not be able to shake someone's hand and greet them by name without you modeling it for her, but do model this behavior if you want her to reach this goal by 8-10 years.

✓ She should not answer the door; this is a parents-only job for this age and younger.

✓ She may have some difficulty shifting tasks and will have difficulty sharing.

✓ She will have inconsistent eye contact with others.

✓ She may not verbally participate in a conversation, or will answer questions with one or two words.

From 6 to 7 years, you can expect your child to do the following:

✓ He will forget your expectations or the rules for how and what he should do when meeting others; you will have to cue him regularly.

✓ He will be able to shake hands and make eye contact.

✓ He will likely answer questions with monosyllables.

From 8 to 10 years, you can expect your child to do the following:

✓ She will be better at greeting, such as saying "Hello" (9+) without being prompted.

✓ She will be better at participating in conversations, provided the topics are concrete, and will respond to questions with more details.

✓ She will be more aware of social cues and agreements between people (For example, she will be adept at acknowledging someone when she greets them at the door.)

From 11+ years, you can expect your child to do the following:

✓ He will be fairly comfortable greeting others and talking to them, especially in terms of greeting people at the door, standing when adults enter the room, etc.

✓ He will be more seen than heard, especially if the conversational topics are not of interest; he will listen, but may not participate.

"Hello, Who's This"
PROPER PHONE ETIQUETTE

You've been here: you call a friend or acquaintance, and instead of a greeting you hear heavy breathing by a very small person, a sudden clank, and background noise as you say, "Hello? Hello?" to an abandoned phone. Want to avoid that at your house? This chapter helps you teach your children the proper way to make and receive phone calls, including giving and taking messages. While you may not get every message someone leaves for you, at least you'll know callers to your house won't be left hanging, literally.

The Basics

Believe it or not, your child wasn't born with a phone receiver stuck in her ear, regardless of how comfortably it seems to fit there now. Young children learn to talk on the phone gradually, under adult supervision. But whether your kids are novice phone users or experienced dialers, the most important things to remember when speaking on the phone are to speak clearly into the receiver in a normal tone of voice (not whisper like a secret agent), use words rather than gestures such as nods or shrugs, and pay attention to the conversation taking place on the phone rather than what else is going on in the room.

If you have really young children you will probably find that they need many reminders to use their words, rather than gestures, when they are on the phone. Remind them to keep using words to respond to questions, and when they are done with the conversation to say, "Goodbye" rather than simply dropping the phone and moving on to bigger and better things.

Basic phone manners covered in this chapter:
* Answering the phone
* Making a call
* Taking a message
* Leaving a message
* Learning to wait while others are on the phone

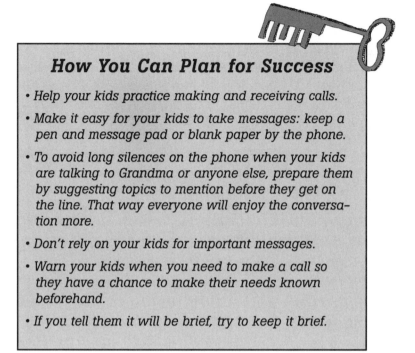

Answering the Phone

In theory, learning to answer the phone seems like a pretty simple accomplishment: it rings, you pick it up, you say, "Hello?"—end of lesson. But for young children it's not as easy as it sounds. Because kids are concrete learners, the task of learning to pick up an object and talk to a disembodied voice, answer properly, and remain undistracted by everything else that is happening in their immediate vicinity is a big job, and one that will require a lot of practice and modeling on your part.

When the phone rings, the person answering it should pick up the receiver and say, "Hello" in a polite, clear voice—not immediately after taking a huge bite of a sandwich or while chewing a pack of gum. If the call is for that child, she should talk directly into the receiver in a normal tone of voice and focus on the conversation rather than the show that's on TV, the project she was just working on, or conversations going on around her in the room. When the conversation is over, she should thank the caller for calling, say, "Good bye" and hang up promptly by putting the receiver back on the phone, not dropping it on the couch or leaving it dangling by the cord.

> *When the conversation is over, she should thank the caller for calling, say, "Good bye" and hang up promptly by putting the receiver back on the phone, not dropping it on the couch or leaving it dangling by the cord.*

That's how it's supposed to work, but probably won't when you're first teaching your kids. Focus on one skill at a time so they have a chance to succeed at parts of a call. For example, praise the fact that your daughter picked up the phone and answered it with a clear voice, and disregard for the moment the fact that she was holding it upside down and talking into the hearing part. Praise what works, gently correct what doesn't, and you'll find that each skill will come in time.

Who's This?

Some parents encourage their kids to identify themselves when answering the phone, by saying, "Hello, this is Kelsey," or "Hello, Wilson residence," which helps callers avoid having to guess to whom they are speaking. Other parents prefer not to have their children identify themselves to unknown callers. Whichever you choose, also be sure to teach your kids caution about providing too much personal information over the phone.

How Young is Too Young?

You will have to be the judge of when your child is old enough to answer the phone. Usually the biggest factor is reliability. There are many distractions on the path from the phone to the person the call is for, and young children who are asked, "May I speak to your Mom?" often forget or become distracted halfway through the trip to find her. A good general guideline is to allow your children to answer the phone when you feel confident that they can be counted on to find the person to whom the caller wishes to speak.

There are many distractions on the path from the phone to the person the call is for . . .

Ask Callers to Identify Themselves

If the caller asks for someone other than the person who answers, the child should ask the caller to identify him or herself. "May I ask who is calling, please?" is more polite than, "Who's this?," which makes your kid sound like a thug.

The child should then alert the person calling that he or she will get the intended person by saying, "I'll get him. Just a minute, please." This also helps young children stay on task; often when asked, "Is your Daddy there?" a child will say, "Yes" and patiently wait for the next question or comment from the mysterious voice. By teaching her to say, "I'll go get Dad. Just a minute," she'll outline the job ahead of her and will be more likely to complete it.

If You Can't See 'Em, Go Get 'Em

If you or the intended person is nearby, your child should put his hand over the receiver before calling for that person, so he isn't bellowing into the caller's ear. For call recipients out of the immediate area, the child who answered the phone should put the phone down and go find the person rather than yelling at the top of his lungs, "Mo-ommm, phone!" A good rule for your kids to use in determining when they should call out to someone versus when they should go get them is that if the person they are trying to find is out of sight, they are officially out of earshot: in other words, if you can't see 'em, go get 'em.

> *. . . the child who answered the phone should put the phone down and go find the person rather than yelling at the top of his lungs, "Mo-ommm, phone!"*

Is Your Mom There?

You will need to establish your own set of rules for what you want your kids to say when you are either not at home, or not available. Many times adults will call and ask the child answering the phone, "Is your mom there?" If you're uncomfortable with your children broadcasting the news that you're not home, or in the bathroom, it's a good idea to teach them to simply say you're unavailable or can't come to the phone right then. This phrase also helps with more literal-minded children, who, when asked, "Is your mom there?" look around and say, "No," even if you're only in the next room. Remember that the younger the child, the more concretely they view life—so if someone calls and asks if Mom is there, they may well answer it honestly—whether it's yes or no—and then simply hang up with a sense of "mission accomplished."

Taking Messages for Others

If the person the caller wants to speak with isn't available, the child answering the phone should say, "May I take a message for him/her?" Have a pad of paper and pencil in close proximity to the phone to make it easy, and remind your kids that a name and phone number clearly printed is fine if they have a hard time writing lots of information down.

If your child isn't old enough to write a name and phone number, you should teach him or her to ask the caller to call back, or if an older child is around, to take over the phone call so the message is properly relayed. Don't expect your children,

especially younger ones, to remember every message exactly the way it was given—how many adults do you know who forget or neglect to give complete phone messages? If you are expecting important phone calls and need accurate information, don't rely on your kids—use an answering machine, instead.

Some families avoid the issue of taking messages altogether by screening phone calls through an answering machine when a parent or adult is not available or not home. That way, if the child knows the caller is leaving a message, he or she can pick up and continue the conversation. Otherwise, the adults can receive messages that come directly from the caller, and privacy and safety are not issues.

Making Calls

When making a call, teach your child to identify himself before asking for his intended party ("Hi, this is Shane. May I please speak with Richard?"). It makes a good first impression, and helps younger children avoid that moment of panic when someone picks up and they forget why and for whom they were calling in the first place. It will also help your child avoid saying, "Who is this?" when the person on the other end picks up, which is guaranteed to make you cringe.

Your child should politely request to speak with his intended party rather than grunting, "Is Richard there?" Older children, especially, tend to talk like cavemen, mumbling into the phone as if every syllable is costing them superhuman effort. This can be very off-putting to the person answering the phone. Speaking clearly, identifying themselves, and then asking for their friend goes a long way toward establishing a positive first impression with the person on the other end of the phone.

Leaving Messages

If your child makes a call and the person she wants to talk to isn't available, she should ask if she can leave a short message. Her message should include her name, the reason she called, and her phone number. If she reaches an answering machine, remind her to speak clearly, and give her name and her phone number with a request to call back. Teach your kids to avoid leaving long, rambling messages on answering machines. It's irritating, no matter who does it.

Call Waiting

If you rely on call waiting, you will need to set guidelines for your children on when calls will go through, and when they can be ignored. You may want to set a general priority scale for calls: incoming calls should take precedence over any conversations your children are having, regardless of who it is. A "kids call back" rule often works well for families with more than one child, or only one phone line. If your children take messages for you on call waiting, the same principles for message taking apply.

When you call 911, they really do respond

Mention "young child" and "911" in the same breath and virtually every parent has a story to tell about how their child accidentally dialed 911 and either the police, the fire department, or a combination of all local emergency vehicles showed up at their door, greeted by a very surprised Mommy or Daddy. While it's very important to teach your kids that 911 is the number to call in an emergency, it's equally important to stress that it's not a number that should be dialed just to chat, or as a test. A great way to reinforce the importance of using 911 only in an emergency is to actually visit your local fire or police departments, and have a uniformed officer lay down the law, so to speak. When your kids hear it from the source they really get the message.

Wrong Numbers

Inevitably your children will dial wrong numbers. Remind them that if they do, they should say, "I'm sorry, I must have called the wrong number," rather than slamming down the phone at the sound of an unfamiliar voice. Demonstrate what you would do in a similar situation, and explain that it happens to everyone. Let your kids know that no one likes a hang up, and most people would prefer to know the caller made a mistake rather than dialed and hung up on purpose.

When Others Are on the Phone

Most parents will agree that the second they pick up the phone, children that were completely absorbed in others things will suddenly have desperate needs that require immediate attention. Fights break out, liquids spill, disasters happen. Teach your child to respect your right to an uninterrupted phone conversation by setting some guidelines about when it is okay to be interrupted. Most of the burning questions your children have for you, such as "Why is there only one slice of white bread left?" can wait a couple of minutes longer. Make sure that you respect their phone conversations, as well. Helping your kids learn to respect your right to have uninterrupted, private conversations will absolutely require modeling that kind of behavior yourself.

You can forewarn your kids before you pick up the phone to make a call, so they know in advance whom you're calling, and about how long it will take. Saying something as simple as, "I need to make a phone call, so please don't interrupt me. I'll be done in a few minutes," is often all they'll need. It will give them the chance to ask that important question before you're busy.

For younger kids, setting up a snack or an activity right before you make a call can be a good idea, provided the activity doesn't require lots of supervision. A bathroom check isn't a bad idea either, especially if you don't have a portable phone; it's remarkable how a bathroom emergency can cut a call short. You may also want to set some guidelines about personal space when you (or they) are on the phone to help make phone conversations more enjoyable. It can be difficult to hear when several people are talking (or fighting) around you while you are on the phone. Similarly, remind your children that taking part in phone conversations vicariously, by interjecting, "What did he say?" or "Did you tell him that . . ." is not appropriate. If the conversation is one that more than one person should be involved in, the participants should either hand over the phone, pick up another extension, or give a summary when the call is over.

And remember that it's really not fair to talk on and on if you've said to them that you're making a quick call. Shushing your children over and over or telling them, "I'll only be another minute," when you really aren't, isn't fair and teaches your kids that whining is the only way to get you off the phone.

Activities and Ideas for Reinforcing Good Phone Manners

Calling All Kids
Age Range: 3 and under

Very young children find the phone a fascinating novelty; after all, they see their parents or older brothers and sisters on it all the time, and it holds great appeal. If you have an old phone, let your youngest kids play with it. Pretend to make phone calls to them on it and let them get used to holding it and speaking into it. Another great way for your young children to practice phone skills is to solicit help from extended family members—they are generally much more patient than the general public, and welcome the chance to have phone conversations with your kids, however brief or bizarre. The more practice your youngest children get, the sooner they'll be comfortable on the phone and be reliable phone answerers.

Sorry, Wrong Number
Age Range: 3 and up

This is a game that will help your kids practice what to say when they accidentally dial a wrong number. No, it's not a license to make crank calls ("Is your refrigerator running? Better catch it!" is still a classic), but it's a way to model the proper response to a mistake. Using a play phone or an unplugged real one, model the behavior you want your child to emulate by creating wrong-number scenarios that you can act out together. Take turns being the caller and the person who answers the phone. This really fun game has a pretty high potential for silliness, but your child will remember how to respond when she makes a mistake.

You Make the Call
Age Range: 5 and up

This trivia game can be played anywhere, at any time. Give your kids phone-calling scenarios and ask them what the correct response should be. For example: "The phone rings, and Mom's in the shower. You answer it, and it's Aunt Marge. What do you tell her?" Kids love to figure out solutions to problems, and you'll be surprised how much they retain from games like these.
Here are some more scenarios:

- ✓ You've just taken a huge bite of cake and the phone rings, do you answer it or let the machine get it?
- ✓ You answer the phone. It's a telemarketer offering you a subscription to a magazine. What do you do?

Cheat Sheet Check List
Age Range: 6 and up

Sometimes even older kids forget their manners. Tape a list of suggested responses near the phone as reminders of what to say. For example, "Hello, this is Richard. May I speak to _____?" may help your older child remember to introduce himself before asking for a friend. Your child will probably memorize the list simply by its proximity to the phone. Here are other ideas for the cheat sheet check list:

- ✓ May I take a message?
- ✓ May I ask who is calling please?
- ✓ Thank you for calling.
- ✓ Just a minute—I'll go get my mom.
- ✓ My dad can't come to the phone right now.
- ✓ I'm sorry, I dialed the wrong number.

No Cold Calls—Phone Scripts
Age Range: 8 and up

Help your older kids practice "scripts" with you before they make phone calls to unfamiliar people or places so they don't panic and need to be rescued. For example, if your child wants to call the video store to see if a certain movie is available, role play a typical conversation with him or her. This kind of practice builds confidence when your child makes the real calls. Of course, you may need to take over the line if the unexpected question comes up, or things get confused, but practicing beforehand will help avoid these situations more than if your child calls cold. This is also a good game to play to prepare for leaving a message on an answering machine.

Questions and Answers

Q. When my son makes a phone call and an adult answers, he immediately panics and says, "Who's this?" rather than identifying himself or asking for his friend. How can I help him avoid sounding so rude?

A. *Keep a script with some key phrases, such as, "Hi, this is _____. Is _____ there?" or "May I please speak to XX?" next to the phone so he can refer to it when he's making the call. You can also help reinforce good manners by rehearsing a little right before he gets on the phone.*

Q. How do I help my children deal with phone calls from other kids at school that are frequent and unwelcome? When do I step in?

A. *You are your child's protector, so the best way to address this is to step in immediately, take the call, and run interference for your child. You can control the situation simply by taking all the calls. It's important for you to deflect the responsibility from your child onto you in this case, since the calls are unwelcome.*

Q. I just discovered that my son and his friend have been crank calling all of our neighbors for fun. Other than getting mad at them (which I've already done), what's the best way to make them really understand how rude this is?

A. *You should have both of them talk to the neighbors about what they've done and apologize for their behavior. The neighbors may not know it was your son and his friend who made the calls, but having the boys tell them they did it will help dispel the idea of crank calls being secret, and will also help them see how they have made others feel. You should also talk to your neighbors to discuss what to say, and to keep the meeting constructive.*

Q. How young is too young to answer the phone? I often call a friend who allows her three-year old to answer on a regular basis. I don't let my own three-year old answer the phone, but am wondering if I should. Any suggestions?

A. *Children under the age of seven are not reliable enough to answer the phone unsupervised on a regular basis. They are developmentally unprepared to remember to take messages, to remember reliably who called and why, and should leave telephone answering to older children. Even seven-year old children should answer the phone under adult supervision.*

Q. My daughter is a toddler and called 911 by pushing random numbers on the phone. The police came and I was very upset and embarrassed. Despite the incident, she still tries to play with the phone. What do I do?

A. *First, congratulate yourself—you're obviously doing a good job modeling behavior, because your daughter is watching and learning from your actions by trying to use the phone—however disastrous the outcome. From all the stories of 911 calls made by youngsters, it's surprising that any real emergency calls get through. So you're not the first, and you certainly won't be the last household to call 911 accidentally. Don't reprimand your daughter, since she's only doing what she sees you do. Rather, buy her a play phone or giver her a real one (unplugged) to play with; and keep the "live" one out of her reach.*

What to Expect

This section is divided into age groups that can be used as a quick reference for what you can and can't expect from your child in terms of answering the phone. You want to have high, but not unreasonable, expectations—otherwise success is sure to elude you. Please note that this is based on very general developmental milestones, and provides general guidelines for children—your child might be much more or less developmentally advanced, and therefore capable of more or less than indicated.

Also be aware that as children move toward the outer limits of the age ranges specified, they will be more likely to have a higher degree of proficiency at the skills listed.

From toddler to 24 months, you can expect your child to do the following:

✓ She will be curious about the phone and enjoy hearing others talk to her on it.

✓ She will most likely not respond back, even to say hi.

✓ She will likely smile when spoken to.

✓ She may pick up or play with the phone.

✓ She will be watching your behavior and try to mimic it.

From 3 to 5 years, you can expect your child to do the following:

✓ He may try to pick up and talk on the phone.

✓ He will answer questions with monosyllabic answers such as "yes" and "no."

✓ He will have no concept of dialing or remembering numbers, but you should begin teaching him and having him practice your own phone number.

✓ He will be unreliable at answering the phone because he will not be able to grasp the needed skills for taking messages or following through (for example, if asked if his mom is there, he may say no, even though Mom is in the next room).

From 6 to 7 years, you can expect your child to do the following:

✓ She will have an increased desire to talk on and be on the phone and will enjoy calls from family members, friends, etc.

✓ She will have some increased understanding of the social rules of the phone (For example, she will be able to go get Mom in the other room if requested by an adult on the other end).

✓ She will not be able to take written messages reliably or remember who called; she should be relied on only to seek an adult immediately when asked.

✓ She will be able to engage in response-oriented communication, and speak briefly about school, her day, her game, etc.

✓ She will likely get distracted (for example by a computer game or television show) and forget she's talking to someone on the telephone.

From 8 to 10 years, you can expect your child to do the following:

✓ He will have an increased number of friends calling and he'll want to call them, too.

✓ He'll be able to write down messages more consistently, but will have inconsistent recall about where he wrote them or what they said—to avoid this, establish a message board and keep it by the phone.

✓ He will generate dialogue with others rather than only responding to questions.

✓ He will have better focus on the phone conversation and will be less likely to be distracted by other things, but not always.

✓ He will need reminders about phone manners.

From 11+ years, you can expect your child to do the following:

✓ She will want to talk on the phone as much as possible for as long as possible, so good luck!

✓ She will be likely to have mastered phone etiquette, but may need some reinforcement through games.

⑤ it's MY PaRtY:
invitationS, commitments,
and the
DREADED THANK YOU NOTe

It's four o'clock in the afternoon, and the party is over. The last guest has gone home, balloon in hand, tracking cake crumbs out the front door. Overall, the party was a huge success—the piñata incident was unfortunate, but your homeowners insurance should cover most of the damage. You're suspiciously impressed with your birthday boy: he was polite and gracious, and behaved exactly as a good host should. What's up?

Do not call your pediatrician. There is nothing wrong with your child—just a terminal case of good manners. Learning the fundamentals of party and playdate manners, from sending invitations to behaving properly at other friends' houses, can make a huge difference in everyone's enjoyment of social occasions. This chapter offers lots of ideas to help you teach your kids the manners they need to be great hosts and guests—all the time.

The Basics

Whether the invitation is to come over to play for a couple of hours or join another family for a fabulous vacation, once an invitation has been extended and accepted, a commitment has been made on both sides. Encourage your kids, especially younger ones, to think carefully before they extend or accept invitations, because it is very hard on the other person if they suddenly decide they want to uninvite their friend or cancel at the last minute.

All of the manners discussed in the rest of the book come into play when your child is a host or guest. Saying please and thank you, meeting and greeting skills, table manners, and respect for others will all be important when your kids have friends over, or are the guests at another person's home.

Basic manners covered in this chapter:

✳ Extending and accepting an invitation
✳ Being a good guest and a good host
✳ Keeping commitments
✳ Giving and accepting gifts
✳ Writing thank you notes

How You Can Plan for Success

- *Review an upcoming social engagement and head off possible problems. For example, are there any toys your child might not want to share? Put those away.*

- *Have a few activities lined up if your child has trouble managing a playdate on his own.*

- *Don't allow your child to accept an invitation if you don't think he can follow through with it.*

Informal Invitations

Usually informal invitations are made verbally, often by the parties involved. You will need to set rules for when it's okay for your young children to make invitations on their own. It's a good idea to require your kids always to check with you before extending an invitation, and for you to confirm the engagement particulars with the other parent either on the phone or in person. That way, you won't have your children's friends showing up at your house without warning if you've already made other plans, and there won't be details that have gone unresolved (or misunderstood), such as when the friend will go home, how he or she will get there, etc.

While older children can work out the details on their own, you should always know how to reach the friend's parents in case of an emergency. Likewise, when your older children are going to a friend's house, they should let you know where they'll be, who they will be with, and how they can be reached.

Playdate Manners

Although your child may offer little information about what she did while playing at a friend's house, you'd probably like to know that she behaved herself appropriately. Here are the three golden rules of playdate etiquette:

✓ Say "Please" and "Thank you" when offered or given anything.

✓ Pick up the toys you've played with.

✓ Thank your friend and her parents for having you over when you leave.

Even the youngest child should be able to manage two out of the three without too much difficulty, and being a helpful, courteous guest makes the visit nicer for everyone. To help reinforce the golden rules, see Activities and Ideas for Reinforcing Good Party and Playdate Manners at the end of this chapter. Remember, too, that the best way to reinforce these basic good manners is to practice them at home.

Make a Parent Pact

It might make you feel awkward at first, but it's important to discuss with other parents the rules of their house, from what is appropriate language, to what kind of movies they let their kids watch. Talk to the parents of your child's friends and come to an agreement about enforcing basic manners such as saying "Please" and "Thank you," toy cleanup, appropriate behavior, etc. For older kids, talk to other parents about such things as what kinds of movies are appropriate for your child to watch. It's better to risk being "uncool" than irresponsible.

Golden Rules for Older Kids

When kids get older, the golden rules list gets a bit more compli-cated. In addition to the above three, older children should remember that when they go to a friend's house, they are not paying hotel guests. That means pitching in to help with clearing dishes, offering to help with jobs that others are doing, and includ-ing others in activities, if there are several kids or younger brothers and sisters around. It's also fine to expect the same when kids come to your house; and you should make it clear that everyone abides by your house rules. Likewise, when your kids are at other people's houses, they should follow the rules of that house. If something isn't okay to do (or watch, or say, or play with) at home, it's probably not okay at someone else's house, either.

Extending Formal Invitations

More formal invitations, such as invitations to birthday parties or other special occasions, are often written and sent in the mail. The invitation should include the occasion, the date, time, and location of the event, and a phone number for responding. When your children reach an age when a written party invitation would be mortally embarrassing, telephone or personally extended invitations are fine, as long as they are delivered with your knowledge and approval.

It's important for kids to remember that if they are having a party and haven't invited everyone, they shouldn't distribute written invitations or spend a lot of time talking about the party to others at school. The only time it is appropriate to distribute party invitations at school is if everyone is invited. Otherwise, use another, more private method. Another option is to have an in-school celebration where everyone is included. That way, your child can talk and be excited about his or her special occasion without the danger of anyone feeling left out.

Accepting Invitations and Keeping Commitments

When someone receives a formal invitation, it is polite to respond in some way, either by phone, e-mail, or a short note, even if the invitation doesn't specifically request an RSVP. It helps the host plan for numbers, and can make the difference between a fun slumber party and midnight madness. If an invitation specifically says, "RSVP Regrets Only," you need to call only if your child can't come.

Once an invitation is accepted, your child has made a commitment to the person who extended it. Encourage your children to view this commitment as a promise that they will follow through and complete, regardless of whether a better offer comes along. Sure, an invitation to go mountain biking is a lot more fun than working on a school project with a science partner on a sunny spring afternoon, but learning to live with decisions and to keep promises is an important, and necessary, life lesson.

You'll need to make the call regarding whether it is appropriate for your child to break a commitment if another invitation comes along, but in most instances you should strongly discourage him from doing so. Breaking one social commitment for another one is hurtful to the person who made the first invitation, and just plain bad manners, any way you look at it.

Being a Good Guest

Party etiquette for guests should follow the same golden rules as for a playdate: your children should say "Please" and "Thank you," help pick up the toys they play with, and thank the host for inviting them. It is a good idea, in general, to discuss very briefly your expectations for behavior or give a quick reminder of the three golden rules before your children go to a party, so they know what you expect of them while they are there.

For younger children, often the most difficult aspect of being a party guest is that they aren't also the recipient of all the gifts. Explaining to them before they go to the party that the gift they are bringing is for a specific friend can help ease the trauma of seeing their gift being unwrapped by someone else.

When the time comes for opening presents, guests should have a hands-off attitude—they should keep their hands off the present and let the host open it. For the youngest children, this can be very difficult; you may find that as the host is opening presents, his guests squeeze closer and closer to watch and help so that the host is eventually buried under a claustrophobic knot of friends. One way to avoid this is to create a "magic circle" around the birthday boy and announce that everyone needs to stay outside the magic circle while the host is opening presents so they can all see and enjoy them.

For older children, being a good guest involves more subtle good behavior. It's likely that some children invited to the same event will not be good friends. Encourage your children to put aside differences between them and their peers, and explain to them that when they are invited to a party, it is their responsibility to be agreeable and friendly to all the other guests, not just the ones they like the best. Most kids are able to do this without much difficulty, and it makes the occasion much more fun for everyone.

Being a Good Host

While the rules for being a good guest are fairly straightforward, it can be more complicated for a young host. Not only is he required to share everything he owns, but the level of excitement can be difficult to manage. It is a good idea to prepare your child for his role as host: go over the activities in the order that you have them planned and make clear what expectations you have for his behavior during the occasion so that he is prepared for what's to come.

It's also a good idea to plan together for possible points of conflict that may arise. Some young children have special toys they won't want anyone else to share, and even the most even-tempered child may be feeling protective or possessive of his personal space and property when lots of other children have invaded it. Talk with your child beforehand about which, if any, special items he might want to put away before the party starts so the potential for conflict is minimal. Also discuss parts of the house that will be off limits to partygoers so he won't be tempted to lead his merry pranksters into the off-limit zones.

Plan For Success

It's a good idea to review as many potential party problems beforehand and head them off as much as possible before the social event. It will help you avoid mishaps during the party, and make things run more smoothly. Here are some things to think about:

- *Identify off-limits areas of the house*
- *Review general house rules, such as no running, no jumping on beds*
- *Keep the partygoers focused on the party*
- *Have a schedule of activities and stick with it*
- *If all else fails, send them outside*

While young children may feel and behave like pampered royalty at a party—after all, it is all about them—as children get older, their role as host evolves from being catered to, to catering to others. Older children should take an active role in making the occasion fun for all of their guests, and should treat all their guests equally courteously and include everyone in every activity to avoid potential hurt feelings among friends and acquaintances. It can be stressful to be the host of a party (and a lot of work!), and you'll need to know when to step in and help your child without appearing to take over. Talk with your older child before the party starts to find out if and when she'll want your help, and exactly what she might want you to do.

And remember that while your vision of the perfect party might be different from what actually takes place, the kids won't notice. Have you ever had your children come home from a birthday party and say they didn't have fun?

Accepting Gifts

It is important to teach your children that accepting gifts graciously is as important as giving them graciously. When your child receives a gift, he or she should thank the giver, open it, and say something enthusiastic or positive, like, "What a nice gift," regardless of how she may really feel about it. This is not teaching your child to lie—it is teaching her to accept the kind wishes of the giver (or her parents) that were extended in the form of a present. Young children often will open a gift and say, "I don't like this," or "I already have one." You can't fault them for being honest, but negative comments in front of the person who has given them the gift will hurt the giver's feelings, regardless of age. Help your child come up with some positive responses to use for presents he or she doesn't like.

About How Much Did You Pay For It?

Another issue that often comes up when gifts are given and received is discussion over how much they cost. Children become fascinated with the value of things around the age of six, and may either ask, or announce, how much the gift they are opening or giving cost. To avoid turning a birthday party into a very surreal, pint-sized episode of the Antiques Roadshow—"This game usually costs about five hundred dollars, but my mom got it on sale for $1.79" — let your children know that discussing the cost of presents, and other items, is best left for family, rather than public discussions.

Leaving a Party

When the party is over, the host should thank each of her guests for coming, and thank them again for the gift they gave. The guest, in turn, should thank the host for inviting her. It's also nice to thank the parents of the host, too, since they'll undoubtedly be more in need of appreciation than the host, herself. Please and thank you go a very long way toward making a social occasion a success, and using good manners when leaving a party leaves a lasting—and terrific—impression.

Thank You Notes

There are few obligations kids (and adults) dread more than writing thank you notes, and for many parents, they may well feel like more trouble than they are worth. But they ARE worth it—not only are thank you notes a way to help your child make a connection with the person who gave them the gift, in many cases they are often the only way the giver knows if the child has received it or not.

Traditionally, thank you notes are written on paper and sent through the mail. Notes composed on the computer, however, can be a viable alternative. While traditional etiquette mavens would most likely pale at the thought, writing a thank you note  on the computer and either printing it out and sending it, or e-mailing it to the giver is fine, and certainly better than no acknowledgment at all.

Much of the tedium of writing thank you notes can be avoided if you and your kids make it fun. The best way to do this is with some advance preparation—make sure your kids have stationery and pens, stamps and envelopes before they get started, or if they are sending them via e-mail, a list of accurate e-mail addresses. It's also a good idea not to try to do all the thank you notes at one sitting, especially if your child has a lot of people to thank. Make a manageable schedule for thank you note writing—even one or two a day—and they'll seem much less daunting. See page 106 for more ideas for taking the tedium out of writing thank you notes.

Activities and Ideas for Reinforcing Good Party and Playdate Manners

"Thanks for the ____"
Age Range: 3 and up

The goal of this game is to come up with appropriate, positive responses when accepting gifts. Everyone writes down three objects on a piece of paper, the funnier the better. Remember to ban bathroom talk before the game begins, or you'll end up with half the slips of paper saying "poopy diaper" or some other inappropriate item. Each person takes a turn drawing a slip of paper out of the hat, then comes up with a response to the "gift." For example, if someone wrote, "old shoe," the gift recipient would come up with a polite response to receiving an old shoe, such as, "Oh, an old shoe! This will match the one I lost in the mud last year perfectly!" It's a silly game, but lots of fun, and it helps your kids learn to be good sports about receiving gifts they may not really like.

Please and Thank You Freeze
Age Range: 3 to 8

The goal of this game is to help make saying please and thank you automatic for your children. While it may take many rounds of "Freeze" for it to stick, this game is a fun way for younger to start learning—and remembering—that please and thank you are the way to get what they want. This works especially well at mealtimes.

Tell your children that you are frozen under a spell, and the only way you can hear their requests for anything is for them to use please and thank you. Usually, kids remember to use please and thank you a few times, then get distracted and forget—until they see you ignoring them, being "frozen." Kids like this game, and you'll like how hard they try to remember to use their manners.

Creating a Magic Circle
Age Range: 5 and under

This activity works equally well for present-opening time, or when the special-occasion child is feeling a bit overwhelmed by all the attention she is receiving from her peers. Stop all activity and announce that the host child has been put under a magic spell. She has a magic circle around her that no one can cross until a certain amount of time has passed (or she's ready to have the crowd pressing in on her again). This way the host can open presents or just get some breathing space.

Create a "Good Guest/Good Host" Poster
Age Range: 6 and under

Younger kids love to know the rules (and police everyone else about them). Before your child hosts a party, help him or her create a poster that has a checklist of good guest and host behavior. Help with the writing, and let him or her decorate it any way he or she wants. You can also leave it up to show guests when they arrive, so everyone is aware of what the rules of this party will be.

Clean Up Race
Age Range: 6 and under

This game serves two purposes: to reinforce to your child—and his guest—that a good guest helps clean up when he's playing at a friend's house, and to get the toys at your house cleaned up, fast. When your child has a friend over and it's almost time to leave, challenge them to a clean-up race. You give them 30 seconds on the clock, and they take turns seeing who can clean up the most toys in the time allowed. They fall for it every time.

Ideas for Making Thank You Notes More Fun, Less Work

Here are some other suggestions to take the edge off writing thank you notes:

✓ Have different colored paper, pens, and decorations, such as stickers and glitter, available to break up the monotony.

✓ Help your kids make their own stationery by tracing around cookie cutters and cutting out shapes.

✓ Turn it into a party—have snacks, turn on some music, and participate yourself. Kids usually work better when a parent is around monitoring them and, ideally, participating.

✓ Help write a template letter they can refer to so that they don't have to re-invent the letter every time.

✓ Suggest that they include a request for the recipient of the thank you note to write back. Kids love to receive mail, and most adults are happy to oblige when requested.

✓ Create personalized thank you notes on the computer using basic clip art or a software art program.

A Nicer Way to Say It

Say you're a nine-year-old kid opening your birthday presents. So far all you've received are socks and underwear, and while you want to be polite and positive, you're running out of ideas. Rather than, "Oh, what a nice gift," for the sixth time, try some of these equally polite, honest, and positive answers:

- *"This is a great color."*
- *"These socks sure will keep me warm."*
- *"Mom, I really needed more underwear, didn't I?"*

If all else fails and you can think of nothing else to say, "Thank you for thinking of me" is always appropriate.

106

Questions and Answers

Q. My daughter sometimes gets "cold feet" before a playdate and I find myself faced with forcing her to go against her will or cancelling at the last minute. What's the best approach—should we simply decline all invitations?

A. *Small steps are key here. Transitions can be hard and anxiety can result from having to spend time in a new or strange or different setting. Make a game of the trip to the playdate. Have your daughter find similarities between your home and the other child's home. Start small—arrange a short playdate of thirty minutes and then leave, gradually increasing the length of the visits over time. If your daughter has not relaxed in the thirty-minute time you start with, consider reducing the time the next time she has a playdate.*

Q. My son's best friend has the most atrocious manners, and I dread having him over. Not only is it unpleasant for me, but his bad manners undermine my efforts to teach my own son good manners.

A. *Modeling good manners and reinforcing how you expect members of your household to behave is always appropriate. You can make a game of noticing other people's bad manners and asking your kids to tell you what the correct manners for that situation would be. Suggest that they prompt their friends, as well. Also, most parents have a "house rules" philosophy, where the rules of the house are the rules for everyone in it, whether they are family members or guests. Make an agreement with the parents of visiting children that you will watch out for their kid's manners and ask them to feel free to do the same with your kid.*

Q. My daughter received a gift that she hated from a family friend. She was very gracious when she opened it, but later told me she didn't like it. We exchanged it for something she loved. The friend recently asked her if she was enjoying her gift. What is the appropriate response?

A. *This is a situation where you should run interference for your daughter: you certainly don't want to teach your daughter to lie, which is what she'd have to do, and you also don't want to hurt your friend's feelings. You should take the lead, give the friend an explanation about exchanging the gift, and let her know that your daughter loves the thought that went into purchasing the gift for her.*

What to Expect

This section is divided into age groups that can be used as a quick reference for what you can and can't expect from your child in terms of manners at playdates and parties. You want to have high, but not unreasonable, expectations—otherwise success is sure to elude you. Please note that this is based on very general developmental milestones, and provides general guidelines for children—your child might be much more or less developmentally advanced, and therefore capable of more or less than indicated.

Also be aware that as children move toward the outer limits of the age ranges specified, they will be more likely to have a higher degree of proficiency at the skills listed.

From toddler to 24 months, you can expect your child to do the following:

- ✓ He will engage in parallel play only, with no real social interactions.
- ✓ He will be unlikely to share and won't engage in conversation with others.
- ✓ He will need a parent or caregiver with him at parties and playdates.
- ✓ He will respond best at a party where everyone gets a gift and adults do the opening.

From 3 to 5 years, you can expect your child to do the following:

✓ She will respond best with a small group of kids; usually fewer than six is an ideal number.

✓ She will not necessarily be willing to share, even if others share with her.

✓ She will be very task oriented; specific, planned activities are good for playdates at this age.

✓ She is most likely to enjoy (and cope with) a party that is very structured, with set games and a limited amount of time (no more than two hours).

✓ She will need a parent or caregiver at parties.

✓ She will need to be reminded of your expectations for behavior throughout the party or playdate (for example, what you expect when she sits down for cake and ice cream).

✓ She will be able to thank and hug family members for presents, but will need to be prompted.

✓ She will not be able to write a thank you note, but you should send one on her behalf with a drawing or her name signed by her, no matter how rudimentary.

✓ She will be able to say, "Goodbye" with prompting.

From 6 to 7 years, you can expect your child to do the following:

✓ He will have an increased ability to share and an increased interest in others' gifts.

✓ He will say "thank you" with less prompting.

✓ He will be excited over games and gifts at parties and is likely to forget manners unless you prompt him.

✓ With assistance, he will be able to call to RSVP.

- ✓ He may not be able to write a thank you note due to fine motor skill development, but can dictate to you (or write one with you on the computer).
- ✓ He will likely enjoy theme parties (for example: skating, swimming, etc.).

From 8 to 10 years, you can expect your child to do the following:

- ✓ She will be able to write brief thank you notes without your assistance.
- ✓ She will be likely to enjoy giving as much as receiving (especially as she reaches 9+).
- ✓ She will be more comfortable with less structure at parties, and will enjoy sharing and interactive play, although theme parties are still a good idea.
- ✓ She will generally make same-sex choices for parties and play-dates at this age, but not always,
- ✓ She will be likely to differentiate between friends and acquaintances and will have strong feelings about whom to invite to parties and playdates. It is a good idea to set a limit on the number of peers and let her decide whom to invite.

From 11+ years, you can expect your child to do the following:

- ✓ He will most likely want to generate his own party ideas and plans.
- ✓ He will have an increased ability to select guests, invite them, and RSVP on his own.
- ✓ He and you will likely feel comfortable enough with his manners and skills to host his party on his own without you helping out.

Quit Kicking my Seat!

manners while traveling

Remember that plane trip before you had kids, when the child in the seat behind you kicked you in the back the entire seven-hour flight, and his brother and sister fought over the sing-along electronic book until the batteries mercifully died? You spent days trying to get "It's a Small World After All" out of your head, and announced that you'd never have children—and if you did, they'd certainly never behave like that.

But here you are! You're planning to travel with your own kids and don't want to go through that experience from the other side. Take a deep breath. Traveling with kids doesn't have to mean hours spent apologizing for bad behavior or worrying about who will melt down first—you or them. This chapter covers the basics of good travel manners, including manners in public places—from extending common courtesies to other travelers to appropriate restaurant behavior—so that with careful planning and some pre-travel coaching, traveling with your children can be something you look forward to, rather than dread.

The Basics

The most important aspect of good travel manners is respect for other people: their personal space, their belongings, and their privacy. Children in public places, including airports, train stations, stores, museums, and hotel lobbies, should behave as if they are guests in someone's home, even if that home offers flights to all major cities and frequent flyer miles.

Basic manners covered in this chapter:

* Moving through crowds
* Using appropriate manners in public venues and crowded places
* Eating out in restaurants and other people's homes
* Conversing with fellow travelers

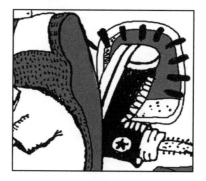

Waiting Areas and Other Public Way Stations

Just as a good guest would use a living room or family room to relax quietly and enjoy being at someone else's house, children should consider the airport, train station, or other public way stations as places for quiet activities, such as reading, chatting, or listening to music. Regardless of their age, it is not appropriate for kids to play tag, wrestle, or jump over seats in any kind of public waiting area. Encourage your kids to find a seat and sit in it. You can play a quiet game together, or if they can't seem to settle their bones, take them for a little walk—go exploring.

While the word "lounge" is often used to describe waiting areas, your children shouldn't take it literally. Teenagers especially find sitting up in a chair very difficult, and usually prefer to slither down until their legs are in the middle of the aisle and their heads are almost resting on the seat. This makes it difficult for other travelers to get themselves and their luggage around them.

Travelers of all ages should use common courtesy when in a waiting area. Luggage should be in a neat pile on the floor next to the traveler's seat if the waiting area is full, rather than on the chair next to him or her, and no one should take up more than one seat if there aren't enough for everyone. You are sharing space with strangers, so be considerate.

If your children are listening to music or playing hand-held games, the sound should be low enough not to disturb other people. If you can hear your child's music through his or her earphones, it's too loud. The same applies to cell phones—it's difficult not to listen in on a phone conversation being conducted less than a foot away, so if your children need to make one last, private call to their beloved before you get on the plane or train, they should find a quiet corner and make it there. Here's an area where you can set a good example!

En Route

No matter what the mode of travel, seats are small and confining, and complete strangers are sitting very close to one another. It's important for children (and everyone else) to sit quietly in their seats, facing forward, remembering not to swing their legs or kick the seat in front of them. If you know from experience that this can be a problem, one solution is to tape a drawing made by your child to the back of the seat in front to remind him or her not to kick. This often helps younger kids remember.

If more than one child is traveling and the potential exists for arguments, too much silliness, or wrestling matches over who gets the window, it's a good idea to separate children as much as possible. Despite their protests that they'd never dream of misbehaving, traveling can get very old, very quickly when you're a child, and any distraction can be a good one.

Remind your children that good travel manners also include keeping their hands to themselves. While the numerous buttons and levers in trains and planes may be intriguing and fun to play with, calling the flight attendant several times, playing with the air or lights, or reclining their seats and then bringing them upright over and over again is inconsiderate to the people around them. Kids like to explore new surroundings, and it's valuable and natural for them to do so. Take advantage of early boarding privileges to allow your kids to check out their seats and the buttons and levers, so that they have a chance to see how they work and what they do.

If children are sitting next to unknown adults, they should know that they don't need to engage in conversation with the adult during the entire trip if they don't want to, or if the adult isn't interested in doing so. You will have to keep aware of the situation, especially if you are traveling with very young children who have no sense of the fine line between cute and annoying, or if you sense your children are uncomfortable.

Traveling with Toddlers: Murphy's Law in Action

You may find that despite all of your careful planning and preparation, your toddler or very young child won't sit still and certainly won't play those quiet games, or behave as you fervently wish he would. Traveling is stressful for everyone, and young children may complain about it loudly to everyone around them, simply because they can. So don't hesitate to intervene and give your child your full attention. Be prepared with drinks and a food treat—after all, who can behave when they are dehydrated or hungry? If your child is spiraling downward in a complete meltdown, getting up for a walk can break the cycle, as well as distract your child. It's unreasonable to expect a very young child to sit still for a very long period of time.

Travel Games—Keep Them Peaceful

While travel games can make the longest trip go faster, your children should avoid the ones that start as fun and quickly degenerate. You and your children should make a list of activities and games before the trip to pull out when the traveling becomes old and your kids are antsy, and you should discuss which games would be appropriate or not. Rock, Paper, Scissors; Truth or Dare; and Uncle, for example, are proven losers in the traveling game department, while I Spy, Tic Tac Toe, and Ghost usually keep everyone happy and violence-free. For a list of ideas and activities to reinforce good manners while traveling, see page 124.

Whatever it Takes: Bribes and Incentives Make for a Peaceful Ride

Call them bribes, if you will, but letting your young children know that good manners en route means tangible rewards is a strong incentive. An excellent way to make the trip go faster and for kids to sit quietly—and happily—for periods of time is to create special travel bags that contain surprises they can open at designated times during the trip. Such items as books, pads of paper, markers, stickers, and other low-tech toys and activities help break up the trip and give kids something to look forward to—as well as occupy them quietly.

Do As I Say, Not As They Do

While you are working hard to teach your children good travel manners, the rest of the adult world could use a couple of lessons. Inevitably you and your children will run into rude travelers, and your children may well wonder why they have to adhere to a set of standards that are obviously not being followed by many of the people around them. Explain to your kids that by using good manners they will be setting examples for the adults around them to follow.

Moving from One Place to Another

Few things other than delayed flights cause more travel rage than trying to move from one place to another in a crowded airport, train station, or city street. It is important to teach your children not just to keep moving, but how to keep moving in crowded places. Just as water flows best when it is moving at a steady pace, eddying and pooling at the edges where it is slower or runs into obstacles, human traffic moves most easily from point to point when people maintain a steady pace in the main corridor and use the edges to slow down or stop.

When walking through a crowded airport or busy street or marketplace, children should stay with parents and travel at a similar, steady pace. If your kids need to adjust luggage, tie shoes, take photos, or just catch their breath, move to the side of the traffic stream, out of the way of other rushing travelers, rather than stopping abruptly in the middle of the action. Travelers in a hurry are often neither patient, nor forgiving, and a businessman late to catch a flight to Phoenix isn't going to care why your child stopped in the middle of the walkway, only that she did—and he won't be happy about it.

Also remember that you are not a marching band. Walking even three abreast down a crowded city street or airport terminal can be inconvenient and inconsiderate to others, especially if the walkers are engaged in conversation, are slower than general traffic, or stop every few feet to admire their surroundings. If your family is a large group, buddy up—it's easier to move through crowds as a pair than as a clot. And if you're worried about being separated, try wearing matching clothes, such as bright-colored T-shirts or the same hats. You might feel foolish, but you'll be easy to spot.

Encourage your children to be aware of the traffic around them, to move with the flow, and to be considerate of others. If there are sights to see or stops to make, move to the side to make them.

Public Venues

When you and your children are in stores, museums, or other public places that require you to move together as a group, remember that it is important for your children, especially young ones, to stay close by. It is a truly frightening experience for both parents and children to be separated in a strange place. If you are in a museum or a place where your party needs to split up to see different exhibits, agree on a common meeting ground and a specific time to meet and check in with each other. Point out to your kids where the information booth is and how to ask for it so they know where to go if they are separated from you.

If your kids are sending you the message that it's time to go, it probably is, even if you're not quite ready to leave.

Remind your children that it is never appropriate for kids to play hide and seek, tag, or other active games in places other than a park, playground, or venue specifically geared for that purpose. If your kids are sending you the message that it's time to go, it probably is, even if you're not quite ready to leave. Part of teaching your children to respect the rights of others is to practice that behavior yourself. If you have young children it's a good idea to limit the number of activities or errands you do in one session so you can avoid this problem altogether.

Also remember to match the activity with the age and interest of your child. Just as you probably wouldn't want to spend all afternoon in a game arcade, your seven-year old isn't likely to be thrilled with the prospect of hours in an art museum or shopping for clothes. Many museums and galleries have low-cost or no-cost activities and tours specifically geared toward kids, or you can create your own venue-specific activity that will interest and engage your kids. Compromise goes a long way toward a fun and rewarding outing.

Eating Away from Home

Part of the fun of traveling is the novelty of eating out for every meal. However, with novelty comes responsibility: whether your children are eating their meals at an exotic restaurant, another person's home, or stopping in for fast food, they should focus much of their energy on proper table manners. All the work you've put into helping them learn good table manners at home (see Chapter 1) will come into play when you eat out. Think of eating away from home as the big game you've trained for all year, or the opening performance of the big show you've rehearsed for night after night. Most children will rise to the occasion with great success.

If you are traveling to a location where the food is unfamiliar to your children, encourage them to be flexible and open to trying new dishes. However, keep your expectations realistic: just because the specialty of the house is jellied eel doesn't mean your kids will dive right in. They will need familiar foods along with new delicacies to keep a balance of comfort and the unfamiliar. A great way to prepare them for foods they may experience during your travels is to experiment with them at home. If possible, make some of the dishes or use ingredients common to the area you'll be going in dishes your children are already familiar with, so they'll have exposure to the new ahead of time.

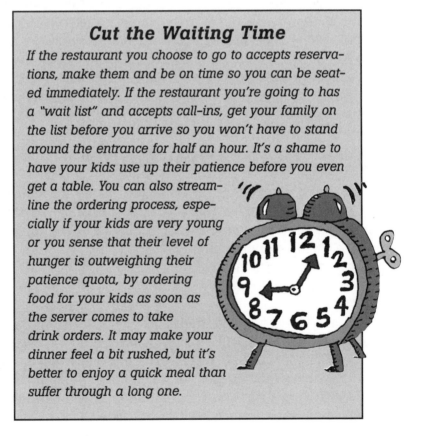

Cut the Waiting Time

If the restaurant you choose to go to accepts reservations, make them and be on time so you can be seated immediately. If the restaurant you're going to has a "wait list" and accepts call-ins, get your family on the list before you arrive so you won't have to stand around the entrance for half an hour. It's a shame to have your kids use up their patience before you even get a table. You can also streamline the ordering process, especially if your kids are very young or you sense that their level of hunger is outweighing their patience quota, by ordering food for your kids as soon as the server comes to take drink orders. It may make your dinner feel a bit rushed, but it's better to enjoy a quick meal than suffer through a long one.

Eating at Restaurants

Many parents think it's cute when their small children wander around a restaurant, playing among tables and visiting other diners. It isn't—that's why people hire babysitters. Unless you are eating at a restaurant with a drive through and climbing tunnels, your children should be with you, at your table, supervised by you at all times. *(See Chapter 1 for more on Table Manners.)*

Part of your responsibility in teaching your children good manners is facilitating the process. Before you even enter the doors, set some ground rules with your kids about what you expect from them during the meal. And be specific: let them know what will constitute manners worthy of a reward (like getting dessert) and what won't. A fun way to keep them thinking about using their best manners is to ask each child what specific skill he or she is going to focus on for the meal. You can turn it into a contest by letting them know that you'll be watching to see who does the best job. You can give the winner a small reward, such as sitting in the prime seat in the car on the way home, picking dinner at home the next night, or perhaps choosing the restaurant the next time you go out.

> ## *Warning: Tired and Hungry Kids Make Bad Travelers*
> *Remember that kids of all ages don't cope well when they are tired, hungry, or both. If you think you can wait "just a little longer" before stopping to get something to eat or take a break, don't. It's better to refuel and recharge before everyone completely loses their cool rather than doing damage control afterward. Bring along small packs of crackers or other easy-to-carry snacks to dole out when you sense a mutiny in the making. It'll help keep everyone's energy level up and you will all enjoy the experience more.*

Ordering Meals

Learning to order their own food is an important skill for kids to learn, and one that helps reinforce their self confidence. It's a good idea to discuss with you what they are ordering before they talk to the server so there aren't any surprises ("Mommy! I'm ordering a tongue!"), and you approve what they pick. If your child isn't quite up to ordering for himself, be prepared to step in and take over so that everyone else isn't inconvenienced. If you have a really insistent child, a good compromise to this is to let him order dessert if he does a good job throughout the meal.

Eating in Someone Else's Home

If you and your children are guests in another person's home, be sure to coach your children before mealtimes about what you expect from them at the table, especially regarding trying what they are served and responding to their hosts. This will be especially important with younger children, whose diplomacy is generally overshadowed by their honesty. A good guideline is to have a "try a bite" rule, where they eat at least a bite of whatever they are served. It will be very important to explain to your kids that regardless of whether they like what they are served, they should make no negative comments or gagging noises and should always thank their hosts for the meal. If food is offered "self-service," children can take what they want without making a fanfare about why they're not eating everything.

Correcting Your Child in Public: Do It Quietly

Kids make mistakes; so do parents, and when you're traveling or in an unfamiliar location, the potential for family stress is high. Correcting your child in public can be embarrassing and counter-productive for both of you. If possible, correct him or her quietly and quickly, then address the situation in private later with an explanation of what went wrong. Younger kids may not remember what they were being corrected for—turn this into a learning opportunity that's light on correction and heavy on pro-active positive reinforcement.

A good way to avoid having to correct your kids for things that go wrong in public is to set positive expectations beforehand, so that kids are cued in to what constitutes good manners rather than worrying about what qualifies as bad manners. And if all else fails, be prepared to take charge and remove your child from the setting if you need to—even if dinner has just arrived. Don't make those, "If you throw one more thing we are leaving" threats if you aren't prepared to follow through with them. You'll lose validity as the authority figure and be tested again and again. "Firm but friendly" is a good motto.

Lose the Tunes

Part of the fun of traveling as a family is interacting with other family members. While personal stereos and hand-held games are great for keeping kids occupied during down time, overuse can isolate the user from other family members, take away from the group experience, and shows a lack of consideration for others. It's a good idea to set limits before you even begin your trip on where and when it's okay to play hand-held electronic games or listen to personal stereos, so that everyone knows what the ground rules are and everyone experiences the trip together on equal terms.

Activities and Ideas for Reinforcing Good Travel Manners

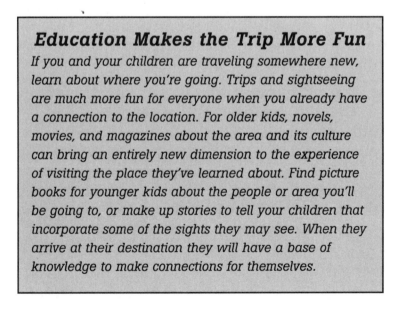 **Restaurant Dry Run**
Age Range: 3 and up

This activity is great practice for eating out, although it will require a bit more work on your part. Your kids will run the restaurant, taking turns at who gets to be the "guest," the waiter, the cook, etc. You will probably be perpetual kitchen help. Have the waitstaff set the table and create a menu for the others, take orders from the guests, and serve the meal or snack. The guest is responsible for good table manners (see Chapter 1) and tipping, while the cook and kitchen help are responsible for preparing the meal. Your kids will have a great time doing this and you will appreciate those nights out at a restaurant even more.

> ## *Education Makes the Trip More Fun*
> *If you and your children are traveling somewhere new, learn about where you're going. Trips and sightseeing are much more fun for everyone when you already have a connection to the location. For older kids, novels, movies, and magazines about the area and its culture can bring an entirely new dimension to the experience of visiting the place they've learned about. Find picture books for younger kids about the people or area you'll be going to, or make up stories to tell your children that incorporate some of the sights they may see. When they arrive at their destination they will have a base of knowledge to make connections for themselves.*

Surprise Grab Bags
Age Range: 3 and up

In this activity, brothers and sisters make up surprise bags for one another. Every hour of the trip the kids are allowed to take out one small wrapped surprise, and open it. This activity not only keeps kids entertained with the loot they receive, but you'll have the added benefit of your kids planning with someone else's best interest in mind. It's a great way to reinforce to your kids the fun of giving things to others.

Determine the number of hours you'll be traveling, and assign each child in your family the job of finding a certain number of small surprises for his or her sibling. You can combine things you already have with purchased goodies. Each surprise is wrapped and kept a secret from the others, so that on the trip everyone is surprised by each item. It can make even the longest trip go faster.

Museum Clue
Age Range: 4 and up

Many museums offer interesting exhibits for young people, but here's a game to help your children stay focused. Choose between five and ten common objects or animals, such as a balloon, dog, car, book, etc. (It's a good idea to be aware of the current exhibits and choose objects they'll be likely to see.) Challenge your children to look at each work of art or exhibit carefully and see if they can spot these objects. You'll be surprised at how engaged in the search your kids can become.

Geography Bee
Age Range: 5 and up

In this game, players must come up with proper place names based on the last letter of the place name said before their turn. The first person chooses a place—"Alaska," for example—and the next person must come up with a place name that starts with the last letter of the word before it. So the second player in this round would come up with a place name that also starts with "a." No place name can be used twice.

✪ *Cruise Director for a Day*
Age Range: 8 and up

Empower your kids! Let each child research and choose at least one activity on your trip, or if you're on school vacation and desperate for diversion, let your kids take turns being entertainment director for the day. Set the ground rules ahead of time for what's acceptable. Have them research the activity, make the necessary phone calls, and find out costs for whatever they want to do. (You may need to help.) Even if the activity one child chooses isn't what the others want to do, they'll know they'll have a turn to be the Cruise Director, too.

Take a Virtual Trip ✪
Age Range: 10 and up

The best traveler is an educated one. Have your kids research your trip online, map out your route, or investigate potential side-trips, activities, or highlights to explore once you get there. Sometimes the most interesting sights aren't found in standard guidebooks, but may be on the Web.

✪ *Take Out Picnic*
Age Range: All Ages

Sometimes eating at a restaurant just isn't going to work. Try a picnic—you'll still get to enjoy the local food and atmosphere. Eat in your hotel room, outside the museum, or in a park.

Are We There Yet?

Long car trips can bring out the whiny inner child in all of us, but by planning ahead you can forestall the inevitable arguments among your kids over who is taking up the most space, and why they can't sing, "99 Bottles of Beer on the Wall" just one more time. Here are some ideas to keep everyone happy and well-mannered when you're on the road.

Bring a good book

If your car has a tape or CD player, try renting or borrowing audio books from the library that the whole family will enjoy listening to—the time can fly by for your kids when they are engrossed in a good story.

Break it up

Plan plenty of stops to break up the trip—they will make the trip longer overall, but your kids will need breaks to stretch their legs. And while visiting the world's biggest ball of wax may not sound like fun to you, your kids will remember it forever.

Play Some Games

These games are oldies but goodies—they worked when we were kids, and should help keep most children appropriately occupied while the miles roll by.

GHOST

In this game, players take turns adding letters together that almost, but not quite, make up a word. (For example, the first person might say, "P", the second might say, "O", and the third might say, "R,". All these letters are part of a real word, but not quite a word on their own.) If a player inadvertently spells a word, she gets a "G" (then an "H", "O", and so on). Players can also challenge each other—if someone is spelling "MTZQ", for example, they probably don't really have a word in mind. If the person challenged can't come up with a plausible answer for the challenge, she receives a "G". The player who gets "GHOST" first, loses.

Anagrams

Choose a word (or phrase) that has at least seven letters in it and see how many other words your kids can make from it. You can choose words that have relevance to your trip. For example, "Rest Area Ten Miles" or "Road Construction Ahead: Expect Delays."

Twenty Questions

Players take turns thinking up a famous person, an animal, or other agreed-upon topic. Other players can ask questions about the topic, trying to obtain enough clues to make a good guess. The player who is "it" can only answer "yes" or "no." If the other players can't make a correct guess in twenty questions, the person who is "it" gets to go again.

Alphabet Game

Players search for letters on signs, license plates, etc., in alphabetical order. The first person to finish the alphabet wins. There is serious potential for cheating on this game, so be prepared to arbitrate disputes—or play it as a group in a cooperative, rather than competitive, way.

License Plate Bingo

Players look for—and record—how many different state license plates they can spot, as well as how many different kinds of license plates they can find for each state. You can do it with a time limit, or for the duration of the trip.

Questions and Answers

Q. When we are traveling, my kids see other children running all over the airport waiting area and don't understand why I won't let them. What's a good way to explain this to them?

A. *One of the keys to helping your children use good travel manners is to explain your expectations beforehand, so that both you and they have the same definitions of "good manners." When your kids see other children use poor manners, make a game of identifying what is wrong with what they are doing and having your kids tell you the right behavior. It's also fine to tell your kids that different families have different rules. Games like "I Spy" are good ways to occupy the sometimes tedious waiting time. Also, make sure you give your children lots of opportunities to move around under your supervision.*

Q. We will be visiting friends without children who eat very late. They expect my children to eat with them, but I'm very worried about their manners since it's so much later than they are accustomed to eating. How can I help my kids get used to eating late?

A. *Remember that your kids come first—don't set yourself or your children up for failure by expecting them to do things they can't. Certainly explain to your friends if you feel it is too late for your kids, and plan for success by giving your children a snack or "high tea" to tide them over, or going out for an early evening meal for them. You also have the option of hiring a babysitter.*

Q. We went out to a restaurant recently, and my seven-year old tried very hard to have good manners, while his younger brother misbehaved so badly we had to leave before dessert. How do we address this fairly?

A. *Make sure you tell the well-behaved child how proud you are of his manners, and also be clear to him and his little brother that you know the badly behaved child will get there, too. It's important to externalize bad behaviors and attribute good ones to the child. That means saying to the misbehaving child, "Mr. Mischief really had you bouncing off the walls, right?" rather than berating him for misbehaving. Also, review your expectations for the meal: was he too young to be at the restaurant you chose? Was he too tired to sit through a long meal? Did you stay too long? It'll help you plan better for the next time.*

Another option for next time is to take the badly mannered child out of the restaurant for a walk or car ride (if there is more than one adult), and allow the other child to finish his meal, including dessert. A quick stop at a convenience store for a treat for your older child is another reward.

What to Expect

This section is divided into age groups that can be used as a quick reference for what you can and can't expect from your child in terms of manners while traveling and in public places. You want to have high, but not unreasonable, expectations—otherwise success is sure to elude you. Please note that this is based on very general developmental milestones, and provides general guidelines for children—your child might be much more or less developmentally advanced, and therefore capable of more or less than indicated.

Also be aware that as children move toward the outer limits of the age ranges specified, they will be more likely to have a higher degree of proficiency at the skills listed.

From toddler to 24 months, you can expect your child to do the following:

✓ She will be active, curious, and anxious if you are; she will pick up your physical and emotional cues, so if you are a calm and happy traveler, she is likely to be, too.

✓ She will feel more at ease if the process of travel is explained as you go. For example, "We're in line to get on the plane." Or, "That noise is the plane taking off. We're going up and up!"

✓ If you are flying, she will likely be bothered by changes in ear pressure and will cry. Lemon on her lips will encourage yawn-type facial movements and will ease ear pain. Bottles, pacifiers, and nursing will also help.

✓ She will be happiest if you keep her as close to her usual schedule as possible. Note that traveling from east to west within the United States is often more difficult for young children than traveling west to east, although you may find the opposite is true if flying overseas.

✓ She will need to get up and move around. If you are flying, request an aisle seat. Bulkhead seats on airplanes will give you more space than the standard seat.

✓ If you are on a road trip, she will sleep if you drive at night. She will also do better if you stop regularly.

From 3 to 5 years, you can expect your child to do the following:

✓ If you are flying, he will need help easing ear pain. Chewing gum, drinking, and yawning will help equalize ear pressure.

✓ He will feel more at ease if you talk through the process of the trip with him, including your expectations for behavior, rules at other people's homes, etc. He will need frequent reminders.

✓ He will need a variety of distractions during the trip. Plan to bring books, toys, etc.

✓ He will need to take bathroom breaks before leaving or boarding.

✓ He will have increased curiosity and perhaps anxiety about sitting in close proximity with strangers. Explain your rules about interacting with others aloud so your child and his seat-mate are aware of them.

✓ If you are on a road trip, he will do better if you drive at night, or during nap/rest time and stop regularly.

From 6 to 7 years, you can expect your child to do the following:

✓ She will be very interested in rules at this age, and will most likely help you notice people breaking rules, even while she is breaking them herself.

✓ She will need a variety of distractions to keep her busy during travel.

✓ She will notice closely what you are doing; it is important to model good travel behavior and point it out to her (for example, wait in line patiently).

✓ She will need to take bathroom breaks before leaving or boarding.

✓ She will be interested in where she is going and how long it will take to get there. Help prepare her for it by learning about your destination, how far away it is, etc.

✓ If you are going on a long road trip, she will still do better if you travel at night.

From 8 to 10 years, you can expect your child to do the following:

✓ He will be a better traveler than at earlier ages, primarily due to being used to sitting at school.

✓ He will be a better traveler if he has activities to occupy him.

✓ He will occasionally need to have rules about dining behavior, etc. reinforced but will be better about remembering them himself.

✓ He will sometimes be able to eat later with adults, but shouldn't be pushed or expected to.

✓ He will likely have difficulty adjusting to time changes from east to west in the U.S. (as children of all ages may); it's a good idea to push back his bed time slowly over the course of a week to adjust, but expect difficulties. Reverse this if flying east overseas.

✓ He will be growing very quickly at this age and may need to get up and stretch, make frequent stops, etc.

From 11+ years, you can expect your child to do the following:

✓ She will have mastered the manners discussed in this chapter, but may need to have them reviewed before traveling.

✓ She will be more socially appropriate and engaged with others and will grasp the concepts of talking with strangers on planes and in other social situations.

✓ She will understand the need to sit and act appropriately when in confined traveling spaces, but may need to move around. (This is especially true of boys of this age who grow rapidly.)

We Rule! You Drool! Go Team!
🏈 Manners on the Field ⚽

You are with an old friend, watching her daughter's basketball game, agonizing over the final seconds. Her team is down by only one point, and the clock is ticking down. Your friend's daughter is running up and down the court, obviously having the time of her life. She gets the ball. Almost no time left. She looks to pass, but no one is open. She steadies herself, and shoots from way out—an impossible shot. The ball arcs through the air just as the final buzzer sounds, hits the rim and bounces off. No goal. The other team wins. The home crowd groans, and you feel terrible for her. You and your friend get ready to go comfort her, for you're sure tears will be coming. But instead of crying she immediately jogs over to the other team, congratulates each of the players, and is surrounded by her own teammates who give her hugs and high fives for her efforts and near success. They head back to their side of the court and gather around their coach, who tells them they did a great job, had a lot of fun, and he hopes that they try that hard every game. Everyone is tired but happy, and they had a great time.

What is this, some kind of Afterschool Special? No, it's just good manners on the playing field—and youth competition at its best. This chapter will help show you how to teach your children the basics of good sportsmanship, from respecting other players to winning and losing with dignity.

It's a difficult job teaching your kid to be a good sport these days. After all, if you look at the newspapers or watch TV, the people who get the most press—and money—certainly seem to be those who behave exactly like the kind of kid you're trying NOT to raise. But it is important to teach your kids to be good sports. In fact, learning good sportsmanship is as important as training to be a good athlete, drama star, or spelling bee champ, because while your kids' competitive careers may last only a few years, good sportsmanship is something they'll need every day, from now through adulthood.

How You Can Plan for Success

- *Set a good example: don't criticize or question the coach, refs, your child's teammates, or your own child.*

- *Keep things in perspective, and don't get too caught up with winning and superior performance. Your children are participating and competing for themselves, not you.*

- *Make it a priority to get your kids to practices and games—on time. Keeping commitments and being on time are important life skills, and this is a perfect opportunity to teach these skills.*

The Basics

Good manners in the competitive arena are all about respect: respect for the team and being part of it, respect for what referees and coaches are trying to teach, and respect for opponents. Competition is like a supercondensed version of real life—everything is taught by example and repeated over and over again in short bursts of time. That's why it's important to make respect for others the keystone of what you teach your children. If you are entrusting your kids to other coaches, make sure you know and are comfortable with that coach's philosophy before you let your kids be coached by him or her. Remember that your child will learn what he sees, and if the coach's philosophy toward the game differs from your own, think carefully before you turn your child over to his or her teaching.

Basic manners covered in this chapter:

＊ Learning to respect coaches, teachers, teammates, and officials

＊ Keeping a positive attitude

＊ Keeping commitments

＊ Winning and losing with dignity

＊ Maintaining good sportsmanship on the sidelines

Teaching Teamwork: Create a Positive Environment

Learning to be part of a team means learning to respect others. The best way to do this is to create an environment where only positive comments and actions are allowed, any time.

Good manners on the field means supporting teammates all the time.

Teaching your children good manners on the field begins with teaching them to be a part of a team—and that means supporting their teammates all the time. There will always be a mix of kids on a team, some who naturally excel, some who are completely clueless, and some in between. The kids who are good will undoubtedly get frustrated with the kids who aren't, especially if a game or competition is on the line. But regardless of the situation, players should not get in the habit of criticizing their teammates.

A big part of the reason that players need to support each other at all times is to foster risk taking. Part of playing youth sports or taking part in any group activity is to encourage kids to go out on a limb and take a risk, whether it's taking a first free throw, trying to steal an extra base, or trying out a new dive. Risk taking requires trust between teammates, and in order to leave their safety zone, kids have to feel that they are supported by their peers. A "positive comments only" environment fosters risk taking and lets kids push themselves.

136

It should go without saying that members of a team should never ever criticize coaches, judges, or referees—but unfortunately, it doesn't. If your child is on the sports field or in a competition, she should never argue a call or make negative comments or even physical signs that she disagrees with what the coach tells her, or, in a competitive situation, what a judge or referee has ruled. Refs and judges have a lot of responsibility and must make quick decisions based on what they see. Boos, yelling, and temper tantrums will not change their ruling, so everyone—players, coaches, and spectators—should accept their decisions with grace, or at least without a fit.

If You Are the Coach

You have a dual responsibility when you take on the role of coach. You may think that setting a good example at home is work enough, but it's even more important on the field. When you're the coach of a team of children, you'll have anywhere from a few to a few dozen children watching—and learning from—your every move. It's vital to behave at all times the way you want the kids you're coaching to behave. You'll need to model good manners every minute you're a coach, from the time you put that whistle around your neck on the first day to the final hotdog you turn on the grill at the team cookout. They don't call you "Coach" for nothing.

Whether you are the coach or not, teaching your kids to accept and support the people on their team will go a long way to teaching them to accept and support people in other areas of life, as well.

Establishing a no-criticism policy and enforcing it really works—it helps keep a positive attitude working all the time on the field, it bonds the team, and helps kids realize that a big part of success is measured by how well they can work together rather than how many points they score individually. Whether you are the coach or not, teaching your kids to accept and support the people on their team will go a long way to teaching them to accept and support people in other areas of life, as well.

As coach, it's important to teach your players to listen and respond to your authority. Try this team challenge. On the first day of practice, when your players are out on the field or court warming up, blow your whistle or call them in. You'll probably find they straggle in one by one, after they've kicked a last ball

Keep It Fun

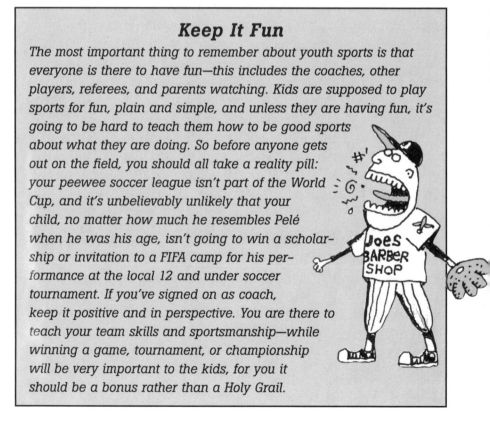

The most important thing to remember about youth sports is that everyone is there to have fun—this includes the coaches, other players, referees, and parents watching. Kids are supposed to play sports for fun, plain and simple, and unless they are having fun, it's going to be hard to teach them how to be good sports about what they are doing. So before anyone gets out on the field, you should all take a reality pill: your peewee soccer league isn't part of the World Cup, and it's unbelievably unlikely that your child, no matter how much he resembles Pelé when he was his age, isn't going to win a scholar-ship or invitation to a FIFA camp for his per-formance at the local 12 and under soccer tournament. If you've signed on as coach, keep it positive and in perspective. You are there to teach your team skills and sportsmanship—while winning a game, tournament, or championship will be very important to the kids, for you it should be a bonus rather than a Holy Grail.

or shot a last basket. When the last players join the group, explain that your signal is their guide—when you call them in or blow the whistle, they should stop what they are doing immediately and run to you. Then send them out again, and blow the whistle again. This time, the last player in has to do a little forfeit, such as two pushups. The kids will get excited about the challenge; no one wants to be the last one in and do the forfeit. This also helps you establish who is in charge on the field, which is an important first step in teaching your team respect.

Teaching and Coaching with the Sandwich Method

One of your main roles as coach is as teacher—you'll be helping your players learn new skills and practice familiar ones, and part of this will involve constructive criticism of your players. You are the only person on the field who should make any kind of critical comment whatsoever to your players, and you'll need to make that abundantly clear to your team. The best way to provide constructive criticism is through the "sandwich method," where you provide positive feedback about an aspect of the player's skill, sandwich in a teaching point for her to work on, and follow it up with positive encouragement.

The sandwich method works for social skills as well as athletic skills. If you need to work on a player's attitude, pull her over to the side and use the same kind of process: "Ginny, I really like the enthusiasm you have on the field. Remember that we only use positive cheers on our team, even toward the other team. I'm counting on you to lead them!" Ginny will go off having heard something positive as the last thing and having been given a special assignment. At the same time, you've established yourself as the leader and the boss, all with positive comments.

Winning and Losing With Dignity

Teaching kids how to win and lose with dignity sounds like an oxymoron, doesn't it? If you've ever played Monopoly with a seven-year old and accidentally won, you're guaranteed to regret it. But it's very important (and actually easier) to teach a team to win and lose with good humor and humility. Part of this is due to the example set by parents and coaches. It's also the positive peer pressure kids can exert on each other—when one kid is being a good sport, he or she influences the others. Another part is creating a spirit of teamwork among players and the sense of responsibility they'll feel to maintain that team spirit.

Inter-squad scrimmages, games, meets, or other competitions are important opportunities to practice winning and losing. As some team members will have won and some will have lost, there can be a discussion about how it feels to be on both sides. Players can see that as good as it feels to win, it feels just as bad to lose—and that's why it's important not to scream and jump all over the field, rubbing a win into another team's face, or stomp, sulk and behave like a two-year old on a bad day when they lose. Kids generally are surprisingly sensitive to other kids' feelings, especially when they have a taste of both victory and defeat.

How to Be a Great Sports Role Model

Competition, whether it is in sports, academics, or the creative arena, brings out the best—and often the worst—in people. If you want your children to learn to be good sports, it is absolutely vital that you model good sportsmanship yourself. Here is a checklist of things to think about the next time you are at a game or other competition:

✓ Do you sit quietly on the sidelines even if you think the ref or the coach isn't doing a good job?

✓ Do you let the coach do the coaching during the games, even if you have some pointers you think would help your child?

✓ Do you support the decisions and advice your child's coach gives her, even if it's not necessarily what you'd recommend?

✓ Do you keep a "positive comments only" rule at your house when talking about other players or coaches?

✓ Do you keep winning and losing in perspective?

✓ Do you remember that after all, it's only a game?

If you answered "Yes" to the above questions, congratulations! You are the perfect sports parent. You're helping your child learn good sportsmanship by supporting the coach's and ref's decisions and by exhibiting to your child that you trust the experience of the coach and her ability to lead and nurture her team. You're also reinforcing to your child the respect you have for the integrity of teamwork and positive mental attitude, and you're keeping winning and losing in perspective.

If you answered "No" to any of these questions, you may need to reassess your motivations. Youth sports shouldn't be an opportunity for parents to relive their thwarted athletic ambitions through their children. Remember that when your kids play soccer, baseball, run track, join the swim team, whatever—it's not all about you, in fact, it shouldn't be about you at all. It's all about them and what they get out of it. One of the biggest benefits is the skill development they obtain from participating—winning is the potential bonus.

Good Manners Means Keeping Commitments

Part of being on a team is making the commitment to it, and when kids don't show up it hurts everyone. It's important to the team, especially as kids get older, that players make practices and games on time and come ready to play. Of course there will be times when your child must miss practice or a game, or will be late, but letting the coach know ahead of time will help mitigate the confusion and potential consequences of absent kids. This works on both the parent and child end: it's important to teach your children that joining a team means making a commitment. Going to practice shouldn't be contingent on what's on TV, or on a preference for scooter riding that day.

Activities and Ideas for Reinforcing Good Manners on the Field

(Note that many of these games work equally well at home, with a team, or even in the classroom. You could also use them at birthday parties.)

"Do This, Do That"
Age Range: 5 and up

This game, a variation on the game "Simon Says," helps your kids learn to pay attention to what you say as well as what you do. Whenever you say, "Do this," the players should copy whatever movement you make. When you say, "Do that," players shouldn't follow your lead. Kids love this game, and it's a good way for them to focus on you and what you're doing, as well as listen and absorb directions aurally.

Last One In
Age Range: 5 and up

This game teaches kids to listen to and respect their coach. It's useful when you want to make a teaching point during practice, or sense that the group is becoming distracted by other things. Call, "Last one in gets caught!" and all your players should run toward you. The last one in has to pay a small penalty, like doing two jumping jacks.

Freeze!
Age Range: 5 and up

This game helps to keep players paying attention to the coach and authority at all times. During drills such as dribbling, passing, shooting, etc., yell, "Freeze!" Players should stop in their places and freeze. If anyone keeps moving because he or she didn't hear or didn't pay attention, give that player a small but fun penalty, like hopping three times on each foot.

Passing the Squeeze/Silent Drills
Age Range: 5 and up

This is a great drill for the end of practice, or anytime you want to calm down your players. Have everyone sit in a circle and hold hands. One person starts by squeezing the hand of the person to her right; that person squeezes the hand of the person to her right, and so on until the squeeze goes all the way around the circle. You can see how quickly you can pass the squeeze from first to last, or break into teams and race. You can add variations such as silent drills to passing the squeeze that help your players learn to learn by observation: players signal to their teammates when they are ready to start the game without speaking or making a sound. This drill helps players focus on working like a team to accomplish a goal. An added bonus is that it's nice and quiet.

Numbers Line Up

Age Range: 6 and up

This game helps kids learn teamwork. It acknowledges and positively reinforces the differences among participants because everyone is equally valuable to the team in the success of this game. Gather your group together and time how long it takes them to line up from tallest to shortest. If you don't want to emphasize height—be sensitive here—choose a different configuration like oldest to youngest, or boy-girl boy-girl. They'll feel proud that they accomplished the task, be eager to reduce their time next try, and they'll have worked as a team without even realizing it. It's also really fun.

Peer Pressure Contest

Age Range: 6 and up

A good way to reinforce to your kids why they need to keep a positive attitude when they are part of a team is to have a Peer Pressure Contest. This can be adapted to any sport, but here it is described for sports that involve a ball and a target. Pick one player—it doesn't matter if she is the best or the worst—and have her come front and center. Explain to the team that if she makes the shot (or pitch, or goal), they all get a reward. If she doesn't, the whole team has to pay a small forfeit such as run around the gym, or the bases. Let the player take the shot. If she makes it, have every player congratulate her. If she doesn't, judge their reactions. If they frown or make negative comments, bring them together and go over the situation: their teammate just went out with the responsibility for the whole team on her shoulders and gave it her best shot. Then ask, "Who misses on purpose?" and tell them to think about how the shooter is feeling, rather than how *they* are feeling. After that, instruct them to do their forfeit. Before they line up again, however, each teammate should give the shooter a high five and some positive reinforcement that focuses on how the shooter—not the other players—must be feeling.

Questions and Answers

Q. My daughter is on a team that wins most of its games. While the kids are good sports during the game, each time they win they whoop it up like it's the championship final. This is usually led by the coach, and while I don't want to undermine his authority, I'd rather that my daughter's team showed a little more consideration for the losing team than they currently do. How can I address this?

A. *This is really important, and also somewhat tricky. You should approach this on many fronts. Without criticizing your child's coach, discuss how it feels to lose with your daughter, and encourage her to be empathetic to the other teams. Use positive encouragement to help her win gracefully. Speak with the coach directly and, in a constructive way, be honest about your concerns. If you avoid presenting your concerns in a critical manner, the coach may be more receptive to what you're saying. You might also want to discuss the situation with the Recreation Director or head of the Physical Education Department—whoever is in charge of organizing the teams—to talk about the philosophy they have toward these issues. This will be the person who sets the tone for the coaches.*

Q. I am my son's baseball coach. When he has been coached by other adults in the past he was a model of good manners, but with me as his coach he argues and whines, and neither one of us is having much fun so far. How can I fix this—what should I do to help him (and me) enjoy our experience more?

A. *Children can confuse roles and boundaries. These are lessons we learn in life as we develop. You are his parent first, and he is used to his role with you as son/parent. Reinforce the change that occurs with the different role that exists when you are his coach. Clear rules and consequences for all players will help clarify the role of the coach on the field. Have him run the bases if he whines so that it becomes clear that all players will suffer the consequences of their behavior.*

Q. My daughter's team recently played in a game against another, much better team. The opposing team's coach yelled constantly at the ref, as did some of his players. My team was pretty shaken by the whole experience, and I want to be able to address it. What can I tell them?

A. *Take charge in the moment. As we have discussed in previous chapters, model good sportsmanship. Point out what is not appropriate about the other team's behavior and let your team know how proud you are of their appropriate behavior and actions. Note how poor sportsmanship undermines the meaning of "game." IT IS A GAME first and foremost, and should not be turned into a battle.*

What to Expect

This section is divided into age groups that can be used as a quick reference for what you can and can't expect from your child in terms of sports-related and team manners. You want to have high, but not unreasonable expectations—otherwise success is sure to elude you. Please note that this is based on general developmental milestones, and provides general guidelines for children—your child might be much more or less developmentally advanced, and therefore capable of more or less than indicated.

Also be aware that as children move toward the outer limits of the age ranges specified, they will be more likely to have a higher degree of proficiency at the skills listed.

From toddler to 24 months, you can expect your child to do the following:

✓ He will not be able to play on a team.

✓ He will not be able to share with others very well or very willingly, although he should be encouraged to do so.

✓ He will be self absorbed and self focused, so expect a lot of "that's mine!" behavior.

From 3 to 5 years, you can expect your child to do the following:

✓ She will play in parallel a lot, and will be increasingly likely to interact and play with others, which is the precursor to team dynamics.

✓ She will be both better at, and more willing, to share with others, especially as she approaches age five.

✓ She will be very hierarchical in her approach to play and especially at taking turns. Boys in particular will demonstrate an increased pecking order that can carry up to 11+ years. The key is to model turn taking and sharing, and reward her when she does so. Girls at this age demonstrate these sharing and turn-taking skills better than boys do, since boys are typically delayed developmentally by about 1.5 years.

From 6 to 7 years, you can expect your child to do the following:

✓ He will be very focused on "being best," which is tied to feeling competent and valued.

✓ He will have an increased focus on winning (in sports, games, even in recess play) as his understanding of the rules of the game increases.

✓ He will be very competitive so it is very important at this age that sports play is led by a good coach (i.e., one who does NOT have a "win at any cost" mentality or use ridicule to make coaching points), especially because modeling has such an enormous impact at this age.

From 8 to 10 years, you can expect your child to do the following:

✓ She will be better at demonstrating social skills, but during times of excitement may regress and will need to be reminded.

✓ She will notice that some parents focus only on winning and are hostile or angry at children who make mistakes.

✓ She will be able to listen to and learn from constructive feedback, especially if it is sandwiched by positive comments.

✓ She will still be focused on winning, but she will also view good playing and tolerance for bad calls as rewards, too. Losing will feel like an insult to her competence.

From 11+ years, you can expect your child to do the following:

✓ His social skills and self acceptance will be more solid as he transitions to adolescence. Watch for regression as he will be less sure of himself as adolescence occurs.

✓ He will recognize that he may have "slips" and may consult with you on problems rather than asking you to solve them for him.

About the Authors

Lauri Berkenkamp

Lauri Berkenkamp has four children whose manners are improving daily. She has written newspaper columns on the lighter side of parenting, and her writing has appeared in magazines and newspapers throughout the United States. She is the author of *Fern House: A Year in an Artist's Garden* and *In My Garden* (Chronicle Books, 2001). Lauri lives in Strafford, Vermont.

Steven C. Atkins, Psy.D.

Steven C. Atkins, Psy.D. is a licensed psychologist, instructor, and clinical associate at Dartmouth Medical School's Department of Child Psychiatry, specializing in specific learning disabilities, ADHD, and developmental theory. He holds a Masters Degree in Education from Harvard University and a Doctorate of Psychology from the Massachusetts School of Professional Psychology. His practice focuses on family therapy and community coun-seling, including working with children in area schools on impulse control and social skills development. Dr. Atkins lives in the Upper Valley of New Hampshire.